Cambridge Elements ⹀

Elements in Global China
edited by
Ching Kwan Lee
University of California–Los Angeles

HONG KONG

Global China's Restive Frontier

Ching Kwan Lee
University of California–Los Angeles

CAMBRIDGE
UNIVERSITY PRESS

CAMBRIDGE
UNIVERSITY PRESS

University Printing House, Cambridge CB2 8BS, United Kingdom

One Liberty Plaza, 20th Floor, New York, NY 10006, USA

477 Williamstown Road, Port Melbourne, VIC 3207, Australia

314–321, 3rd Floor, Plot 3, Splendor Forum, Jasola District Centre,
New Delhi – 110025, India

103 Penang Road, #05–06/07, Visioncrest Commercial, Singapore 238467

Cambridge University Press is part of the University of Cambridge.

It furthers the University's mission by disseminating knowledge in the pursuit of
education, learning, and research at the highest international levels of excellence.

www.cambridge.org
Information on this title: www.cambridge.org/9781108823913
DOI: 10.1017/9781108914895

First published 2022

A catalogue record for this publication is available from the British Library.

ISBN 978-1-108-82391-3 Paperback
ISSN 2632-7341 (online)
ISSN 2632-7333 (print)

Hong Kong

Global China's Restive Frontier

Elements in Global China

DOI: 10.1017/9781108914895
First published online: July 2022

Ching Kwan Lee
University of California–Los Angeles
Author for correspondence: Ching Kwan Lee, cklee@soc.ucla.edu

Abstract: How did Hong Kong transform itself from a shoppers' and capitalists' paradise into a city of protests at the frontline of a global anti-China backlash? This Element situates the China–Hong Kong contestation in the post-1997 era in the broader context of "global China," conceptualized as a double movement. On the one hand, Beijing deploys a bundle of power mechanisms – economic statecraft, patron-clientelism, and symbolic domination – around the world, including Hong Kong. On the other, this Chinese power project triggers a variety of countermovements from Asia to Africa, ranging from acquiescence and adaptation to appropriation and resistance. In Hong Kong, reactions against the totality of Chinese power have taken the form of eventful protests, which, over two decades, have broadened into a momentous decolonization struggle. More than an ideological conflict between a liberal capitalist democratizing city and its Communist authoritarian sovereign, the Hong Kong story, stunning and singular in its many peculiarities, offers general lessons about China as a global force and its uneven consequences. This title is also available as Open Access on Cambridge Core.

Keywords: global China, Hong Kong, decolonization, protests, internal colonization

ISBNs: 9781108823913 (PB), 9781108914895 (OC)
ISSNs: 2632-7341 (online), 2632-7333 (print)

Contents

1 Hong Kong as Puzzle

The 2019 protests in Hong Kong marked a pivotal moment for Asia's financial hub, China, and the world. Massive peaceful demonstrations initially opposing the extradition of criminals to China grew into a society-wide uprising demanding full democracy, even independence, from China. For six months, the world was transfixed by real-time spectacles of a global city on the brink: first came several million-strong marches featuring the city's hallmark orderliness and civility, then weekly violent skirmishes between black-clad youngsters and riot police in full gear. As makeshift barricades rezoned the world's most expensive real estates into quasi-war zones, tear gas and flames of petrol bombs shrouded the city's famous neon-lit streets. A new sense of time and space emerged, denoted now by the dates of political suicides, police atrocities in blood-stained subway stations, mass occupations of the airport, a Dunkirk-style civilian rescue of protesters, territory-wide "Baltic Way" human chains, the erection of Lennon Walls built from memo-sized protest messages in every neighborhood, and waves of solidarity protests by the Hong Kong diaspora in different countries.

The ubiquitous sight and sound of "Liberate Hong Kong, Revolution of our Times," the movement's signature slogan, embodied the euphoric sense of people's empowerment unprecedented in Hong Kong's history. Beijing, consumed by its trade war with the United States, watched on, assailing foreign forces for subversive intentions while outsourcing the dirty work of brutal repression to the Hong Kong police. An improbable revolution was gathering steam, only to be halted in 2020 first by a deadly coronavirus and then more fatally by a full-throttled crackdown. In the name of a new National Security Law, Beijing terrorized and demolished the city's liberal institutions – the media, education, legislature, election, the common law court, and more. Months of mass arrests and political persecutions roundly uprooted several generations of democratic political leadership. By 2022, Hong Kong's status as a free and liberal haven has all but unraveled. But as Hong Kong fell, the West geared up for staunch condemnations and sanctions against China's violation of human rights. A so-called new Cold War has begun.

How did Hong Kong transform itself from a shoppers' and capitalists' paradise into a city of protests at the frontline of a global backlash against China? Most analysts frame the struggle between Hong Kong and Mainland China as an ideological and political one, pitting liberal capitalist democracy against Communist authoritarianism. Some China observers and Beijing officials alike pointed to Hong Kong protesters' rebellious provocation as the culprit for bringing about the National Security Law and its aftermath.

Others spotlighted Xi Jinping's outsized personal political ambition and intolerance for dissent. Yet, this Element adopts a global China perspective and argues that what happened to Hong Kong in the past two decades is part of China's interventionist and repressive turn toward the world at large, a turn driven by systemic political economic imperatives, and augmented by incidental and individual factors. The global China project has subsequently triggered a range of locally shaped modalities of countermovements, including popular rebellions such as those in Hong Kong. Simply put, to understand Hong Kong's rise as a city of protest is to hold in the same plane of analysis two parallel but contradictory trajectories of development coming to a fateful face-off at a time of rising international tension.

The first trajectory is China's global rise and its outbound deployment of power in three major modes: economic statecraft, patron clientelism, and symbolic domination. Their application to Hong Kong explains why Beijing veered from a five-decade-long policy of preserving Hong Kong's autonomy and difference toward ever more autocratic control. The second trajectory developing in tandem and in contradiction to the first is a two-decade-long process of decolonization from below. Manifested as the radicalization and politicization of a city, especially its younger generations coming of age in an era of digitized transnationalism, a politics of belonging energized waves of protest movements targeting Chinese domination. As the Hong Kong citizenry leveraged the city's global capacity for resistance, taking historicity into their own hands in a place-making project, they also ran afoul of the Chinese Communist project of enhanced domestic securitization in anticipation of external international challenges.

Like a double helix, global China and global Hong Kong are two spiraling structures that intersect and entangle, yet each has its own generative dynamics. The Sections 2 and 3 delve into each of these dynamics. But the Hong Kong story, stunning and singular in its many peculiarities, also offers general lessons about a global force and its uneven consequences, as the conclusion will discuss.

1.1 Conceptual Tool Kits: Hong Kong Studies and Global China Studies

"Why and how did Hong Kong become the restive frontier of global China?" is puzzling because neither Hong Kong studies nor Global China studies offer ready answers. Seminal works on Hong Kong have mostly adopted structural and institutional perspectives that explain its political apathy and weak capacity for civil society activism, both under British colonialism and Chinese sovereignty. These key texts are not wrong but partial, as they fail to appreciate the role of "events," "global city politics," and "political generations" in transcending and transforming political and economic structures. A similar bias toward structural power characterizes the literature on global China, obscuring how different forms of resistance and negotiations (i.e. what Karl Polanyi termed "countermovements"), have all along been constitutive of China's expansion overseas. These theoretical categories should be in the tool kits for both fields of inquiry.

1.1.1 Hong Kong Studies

Throughout its history as a trading entrepôt, manufacturing base, regional transport hub, and global financial center, Hong Kong's economy looms larger than its politics and social development in the global and local imagination, as well as in popular and academic writings of the city. The cliché went that Hong Kong – as a borrowed time and borrowed place under British colonial rule, perched on the southeastern border of Communist China – had nurtured a materialistic society allergic and apathetic to politics or ideology. The most influential theorization of the absence of politics in the colonial era is Lau Siu Kai's (1982) concept of a "minimally integrated social political system." Offering a *structural* explanation for Hong Kong's political stability, he argues that, under British rule, an autonomous bureaucratic polity and a materialist, pragmatic, apolitical, family-centered Chinese society were compartmentalized and depoliticized. Between the polity and society were a consensus on the primacy of political stability and economic prosperity, mechanisms of co-optation of a Chinese elite into the political establishment dominated by a British generalist-administrative elite, and "boundary politics" involving minor adjustments of public policy or redistribution of resources without popular demands for the restructuring of the system. A key condition for the perpetuation of this minimally integrated sociopolitical system was China's endorsement and its interests in maintaining Hong Kong's status quo as an open economy under British rule.

The rise of a new generation of scholars and the sea change in Hong Kong's sociopolitical development have led to revisions and rejections of Lau's interpretation of Hong Kong's past and present. Instead of non- or minimal intervention by the colonial bureaucracy, scholars argued that, from the 1950s to the 1970s, the colonial regime's interventions took many forms. Hidden state subsidies such as public housing, provision of education and medical care, rent control, and price negotiations for foodstuffs imported from China, amounted to social wages that contributed significantly to capitalist accumulation and Hong Kong's economic takeoff as a low-cost manufacturing center (Schiffer 1991). Such state intervention in the economy shatters the myth of Hong Kong as a text-book case of a laissez-faire economy. Elsewhere, Chiu and Hung (1999) showed active government interventions in the New Territories in the 1950s and '60s in order to secure support of rural interests to its rule.

Lam Wai-man's *Understanding the Political Culture of Hong Kong* (2004) mounts an effective critique of Lau's claim of political indifference. She shows that Lau uses a narrow definition of political participation, as acts seeking to influence government policies through formal channels. Excluding practices such as participation in social movements, demonstrations, and strikes, Lau fails to note and account for significant incidents of collective mobilization, protests, and riots in the post–World War II period up to the 1970s. Instead of mundane boundary politics, Beijing, Taipei, and the Hong Kong government, each with their own networks, activists, and organizations, were the instigators and targets of Hong Kong people's political activism. Yet, even Lam concedes the existence of a "culture of depoliticization" underpinning the political apathy among the majority of Hong Kong citizens.

As Hong Kong entered the transition (1984 to 1997) and then the postcolonial periods, politics emerged as a central focus of Hong Kong studies. Multiple governance crises after 1997 had rocked a political system still in flux, and Beijing had frozen the democratization timetable promised in the Basic Law, the city's mini-constitution. Ma Ngok (2007) explains the slow process of democratization after 1997 using an institutional perspective:

> A fragmented state elite and fragmented state institutions after 1997 failed to provide effective governance and leadership. The underdevelopment of political society made it difficult to bridge the gap between state and civil society, channel public opinion, aggregate interests or mediate conflicts. The gap between the political society and the civil society also disabled a strong democratic or social movement to push social and political reforms. (2007: 7)

According to Ma, these institutional weaknesses and contradictions have multiple sources. One is Beijing's institutional design for Hong Kong which, while executive-centered, prohibits the formation of a governing party. The governing elites are co-opted from different sectors with little unified vision, social support, or mobilization power. The arrested development of political parties is also due to the institutional setup structurally designed to give legislators, most of whom are not directly elected, limited policy influence. Even with a high level of civil liberty and freedom of association, civil society is alienated from but vocally critical of the government and political parties, and lacks internal solidarity to constitute a sustainable political force.

These structural, cultural, and institutional perspectives together portray Hong Kong as a bustling global commercial and financial metropolis, with politics a second thought and secondary concern. Yet, these studies have ignored an important fact: in Hong Kong's otherwise calm ocean of routinized, rule-binding political (in)activity and apathy, Hong Kong citizens had time and again joined sudden outbursts of mass political action. In extraordinary, eventful moments such as the 1966–7 riots, the 1989 pro-Tiananmen rallies, the July 1, 2003 rally, the 2014 Umbrella Movement, and the 2019 anti-extradition protests, Hong Kong citizens have demonstrated their impressive capacity for passionate and daring expressions of political activism that caught the world by surprise. Some of the recent protests have inspired an academic cottage industry applying the concepts of social movement theories to Hong Kong (e.g. Lee and Chan 2011, 2018; Cheng and Yuen 2018; Ma and Cheng 2019). But in departing from earlier deterministic structural and institutional analyses, these social movement studies go to the other extreme of narrowly focusing on the process of mobilization itself, leaving unanswered important questions such as the sources of changing political orientations among citizens or how social structure and political economy shape the aims and contents of the movements (cf. Walder 2009). In using a universal set of concepts to all movements without regard to their nature, goals, and historical contexts, these Hong Kong social movement studies fail to explain the totality and historicity of Hong Kong as a city of protests.

In this Element, I seek to reinstate in a nondeterministic way the political economic forces (i.e. the advance of global China, the politics of global cities) that transform Hong Kong society and its politics, with due attention to the capacity of collective agency (i.e. political generations) to seize political spaces within or break out of structural and institutional constraints (i.e. eventful protests), to build a broadening countermovement that, over time, grew into a decolonization struggle against China. First, some brief notes on "events," "global city politics," and "political generations" – analytical categories that have hitherto been downplayed in Hong Kong Studies.

"Events" are concentrated moments of political and cultural creativity when the constraints imposed by history and structure are reconfigured by human action but by no means abolished (McAdam and Sewell 2001: 102). The concept of event is particularly illuminating for understanding Hong Kong politics and society. Despite being under the sovereign control of the world's most formidable authoritarian regime, citizens have managed to pull off one energetic mass protest after another. More than just allowing for contingency in history, "events" as a theoretical category points to mechanisms that bring about change. "Events transform structures largely by constituting and empowering new groups of actors or by re-empowering existing groups in new ways," putting in motion social processes that are "inherently contingent, discontinuous and open ended" (Sewell 2005: 110). The transformative capacity of events lies in the mechanisms of social change they fuel: organizational networks expand, frames are bridged, new cultural categories and narratives are formulated, and interpersonal trust is consolidated (della Porta 2012). Section 3 recounts how, during eventful political protests, Hong Kong citizens break loose the constraints of structure and institutions to build new networks, narratives, and subjectivities.

Hong Kong has been rightly recognized and analyzed as a textbook case of a "global city," a vibrant node offering connectivity and intermediary producer services to multinational capital with ever expansive networks of operations. Hong Kong's development as a central nodal point in Asia with a concentration of international trading, banking, financial, insurance, legal, and information expertise is a long process dating back to its colonial beginning in mid-nineteenth century as a British trading port but more importantly as a hub for inter-Asia and then China trade (Chiu and Lui 2009). Yet, the theoretical impetus of the global city literature (e.g. Sassen 2001) is capitalist accumulation and the resulting socioeconomic polarization, ignoring the transformation in civic and political culture as concomitants of the making of a global city. In Section 3, we will see how the government's attempts to make Hong Kong into Asia's global city inadvertently stimulate citizens' cosmopolitan political imagination and protest strategies, even a brand of global city diplomacy.

Other than "event" and "global city politics," Hong Kong studies should take seriously Karl Mannheim's notion of "political generations." To Mannheim (1952: 291), "generation" is not a passive demographic location, but "generation as actuality," whereby members have a concrete bond through their exposure to and participation in the social and intellectual symptoms of a process of dynamic destabilization, such as in times of war (Pilcher 1994: 490). Within a generation there are likely to be different units defined by different, even opposing, forms of response to a particular historical situation. The sociologist Tai-lok Lui (2007) has proposed a four-generation framework to explain Hong Kongers' satisfaction or discontents with the status quo. Yet, his conception of generational agency is too narrowly predicated on mobility opportunities and materialistic incentives. Section 3 will show that the post-1997 generations are much more motivated by politics, rights, and civic values in the face of Chinese interference than previous generations. The logic of their responses to these historical contexts has to be apprehended on their own terms.

1.1.2 Global China Studies

Turning to the scholarship on global China, one can note a similar bias privileging China's imperatives and domination practices, leaving analyses of resistance to a footnote. The two-decade-long march of global China (i.e. outward flows of investment, loans, infrastructure, migrants, media, cultural programs, and civil society engagement from China) has left sweeping but variegated footprints in many parts of the world. International reactions to the increasingly ubiquitous presence of China and the Chinese people in almost every corner of the world have evolved from a mixture of anxiety and hope, to a more explicitly critical backlash and resistance. Yet, both academic and journalistic accounts have harped on the sweeping scope and enormous size of China's global presence and grand strategy, interpreting these through the lens of imperialism or neo-colonialism (for a review see Lumumba-Kasongo 2011). Chinese domination has been assumed, rather than demonstrated, and the politics of negotiation, appropriation, adaptation, and resistance to global China has been ignored.

I conceptualize global China as a Chinese state project, entailing a bundle of power mechanisms – economic statecraft, patron-clientelism, and symbolic domination – that Beijing applies unevenly around the world, triggering a variety of responses. These generic modalities of power are deployed by other countries as well but the Chinese way is marked by the visible and heavy hands of the state (e.g. state-owned enterprises, policy banks, united-front bureaucracy, and state-controlled media). Section 2 examines global China in Hong Kong by supplementing extant structural explanations of *why* (i.e. motivation) China wants to go global with processual and political analysis of *how* (i.e. power mechanisms) China has pursued its global agenda, and with *what* (i.e. varieties of responses) consequences. In doing so, I adopt Karl Polanyi's (1944) famous formulation of "double movement" as a heuristic lens to track global China. For Polanyi, the spread of the market in nineteenth-century Europe was a double movement – on the one hand, the advance of the market to commodify resources meant for life itself, and, on the other, society's self-protection movements to subordinate and regulate the market. Global China is a specific kind of state-sponsored marketization, and we should expect a concomitant countermovement. The case of China in Hong Kong and its discontents opens a dramatic vista for grappling with global China as a double movement.

1.2 Arguments

When China resumed sovereignty over Hong Kong from British hands in 1997, the Communist regime used the framework of "One Country, Two Systems" to leverage Hong Kong's difference for national development and integration with the global capitalist economy. Yet, soon after the handover, as Section 2 explains, global unrest against autocracies, followed by the global financial crisis, occasioned Beijing's policy shift toward national securitization and global expansion. Its interventionist and repressive turn toward Hong Kong was part of this grand strategic reorientation. This section details the major power mechanism of global Chinese expansion and how they have been applied to Hong Kong: (1) economic statecraft (using investment in infrastructure and key economic sectors to exercise political influence); (2) patron-clientelism (co-opting local political elites, mobilizing the Chinese diasporic community and social networks to build grassroots power); (3) symbolic violence (using education, media, and public discourses to shape perception and identity).

As more interventions and repressive controls are imposed by Beijing and its local agents, a process of decolonization from below has emerged in Hong Kong under Chinese sovereignty. Section 3 traces how Hong Kong's postcolonial generations seized the semi-democratic political space and civil liberty essential to the city's global financial activities to stage eventful protests in response to China's interventions. The result was the flourishing of "localism," a broad amalgam of political ideas, demands, groups, and tactics advocating Hong Kongers' right to democracy and self-determination. It is the story of a city and its younger generations coming to realize their own political subjectivity through reflexive accumulation of collective capacity in an age of global imagination and action.

Section 4 concludes this Element by locating Hong Kong in a spectrum of resistance and adaptation to global China in Asia, Africa and Latin America. What can we learn about the limits and effectiveness of global Chinese power from the case of Hong Kong?

2 Global China's Playbook in Hong Kong

A key piece to resolving the Hong Kong puzzle as "the restive frontier of global China" is Beijing's interventionist turn toward Hong Kong, spurring popular resentment and resistance. Before 1997, successive leaderships in China tolerated, even exploited, Hong Kong's unique status as a global borderland. In the nineteenth century, this rocky island with a deep-water harbor located at the mouth of the Pearl River Delta in southern China, not far from the transnational trading port of Canton, attracted the attention of British merchants fighting the monopoly of the East India Company. Eager to have a free port for European free trades in China and Southeast Asia, merchant interests began lobbying London to put down the lion's paw in Hong Kong, which eventually became a British possession at the end of the Opium War in 1842. Commerce, not Christianity or civilization, was the raison d'être of Hong Kong as a crown colony. Tumultuous political upheaval in Mainland China, Japanese occupation, and Korean War notwithstanding, the transnationality of Hong Kong's "middleman capitalism" (Hui 1999) remained a constant till this day. Its role as a regional center amidst vast, centuries-old trading networks for both intra-Asian and Asian–Western commerce during war and peace served the interests of many stakeholders and was the material foundation for its unique political and social formation.

It was a major historical irony that pragmatism, not ideology, drove the development of this frontier city between British colonialism and Chinese communism after World War II. Historians concur that Hong Kong remained a British colony for as long as it did largely at Beijing's desire. At several critical junctures, Chinese Communist leaders could have easily recovered Hong Kong by force with little British resistance. But they did not. Whatever nationalistic impulse might have existed eventually yielded to pragmatic concerns for the paramount and unique advantages Hong Kong's colonial status would bring to the Mainland. Mao and his top officials in Hong Kong on the eve of their victory in 1949 declared China's intention not to retake Hong Kong by force or to destabilize the colony by agitating for its return (Roberts 2016: 21–22). A glaring contradiction to their revolutionary rhetoric of anti-colonialism, the Chinese Communist Party (CCP) adhered to a policy of peaceful coexistence when it came to Hong Kong (and Macao), preferring to make "holistic and long term use" of the colony (Carroll 2021). Tellingly, at the height of the Cultural Revolution in 1967, when militant Red Guards and some factions in the People's Liberation Army agitated a military take-over of Hong Kong, Premier Zhou Enlai issued directives to prohibit escalation of clashes at the Sino–British border. Even in peaceful times, China could have wreaked havoc in Hong Kong's socioeconomic life by flooding the territory with refugees or blocking the supply of foodstuff and water across the border.

Britain shared the same pragmatic calculations as China did in retaining Hong Kong as a formal crown colony, even at a time when the British Empire was rapidly shrinking and ex-colonies gained independence in the wake of World War II:

> Losing Hong Kong would hurt British prestige in Southeast Asia, especially after the independence of India, Burma, and Ceylon. Keeping it could be a good way to get support from the United States. With an insurgency in Malaya and the impending Communist victory in China, holding on to Hong Kong became of great psychological importance." (Carroll 2021: 47)

In lieu of independence or self-government, informal devolution of power from London to the colonial administration allowed the latter to continue its rule with a high degree of autonomy. In Hong Kong, colonial governors, known to harbor muted hostility toward their constitutional overlords in London throughout British imperial history, went the furthest. They rejected Whitehall's policy to democratize colonies and impose exchange controls over the Sterling areas in the 1950s, and made Hong Kong an independent player in world trade forums in the 1960s. The colony fixed its own exchange rate, managed its own foreign reserves, and broke its currency link with Sterling in the 1970s (Goodstadt 2009). Through all these, governors were acting to preserve Hong Kong's survival and leverage as a globally connected economy inextricably tied to and affected by Communist China.

Cold War Hong Kong best illustrates how the city functioned as a unique and indispensable nexus among the great powers that were otherwise ideological nemeses. "In Hong Kong the rules of the global cold war were often suspended" (Roberts 2016: 26). Not only was Hong Kong China's only treaty port through which trade and currencies transactions with the West were conducted. It was also the regional base for Asian, European, American, and Chinese banks, and an enclave of spies from both sides of the Cold War. Foreign journalists, CIA operatives, and the American consulate staff met their Chinese counterparts in Hong Kong, which became the most important source of hard economic, political, and military information on Communist China. US-funded anti-Communist publications, filmmaking, NGOs, disaster relief, and refugee services competed with Mainland-sponsored ones.

> Hong Kong was also a locale where mainland Chinese and US interests encountered each other on a daily basis. Had the PRC been sufficiently forceful in its objections to American activities in the colony, in terms of intelligence gathering, anti-Communist propaganda, covert operations, and, during both the Korean and Vietnam conflicts, procurement of war supplies, servicing US warships, and hosting American military personnel on leave, Britain would have had few alternatives but to ask the Americans to leave. This did not happen. In practice, China and the United States reached a tacit understanding as to just how much China might tolerate American usage of Hong Kong as a Cold War base and symbol." (Roberts 2016: 56)

Accommodation of multiple strategic interests among Britain, the United States, and China – even with muted antagonism – allowed Hong Kong to survive and thrive as a distinct melting pot of diverse culture, information, businesses, and political sympathies.

The Chinese policy of nonintervention remained intact during the reform and opening period when Hong Kong's special status made it a premier beachhead for the influx of foreign investment, technology, and management skills necessary for China's thirty-year economic boom. In China's calculation, maintaining the status quo meant inheriting from the British an "apolitical world-class financial hub" that could be conveniently repurposed for China's global ascendance. This is why after resuming sovereignty over Hong Kong in 1997, coinciding with China's decision to integrate with the global capitalist economy and international political order, Beijing had initially and largely adhered to the established policy of strategic tolerance of the Hong Kong difference. What the CCP trumpeted as Deng Xiaoping's visionary framework of "One Country, Two Systems" for preserving Hong Kong's status quo for fifty years actually echoed a similar promise of autonomy that was used to lure Tibet in the 1950s (Goldstein 1997).

2.1 Why China's Paradigm Shift?

Two spirals of turbulence emerging independently in the first decade of the twenty-first century converged to create a perfect storm, swaying Beijing toward an interventionist turn in its Hong Kong policy. First, Beijing's concern with national security grew in the wake of the Color Revolutions in former Eastern European Communist regimes, a half-million-strong demonstration in Hong Kong, rebellions in Tibet, Xinjiang, and the Arab Spring. Second, the 2008 global economic crisis exhausted China's export-led model of economic growth, exacerbated its overcapacity problem, threatened its performance-based legitimacy, and produced enormous pressures on China to intensify its global expansion, including Hong Kong. It is these twin imperatives, not simply the city's governance crisis emphasized in most analyses, that entrench China's ever deepening and tightening grips over Hong Kong as well as Mainland society more generally.

This section first analyzes the nature and origin of these two sets of challenges, pointing to the local, national, and global sources of China's paradigm shift in relating to Hong Kong. Next, we will examine Hong Kong as one of the many destinations where China has exerted its power. The analysis here pays attention to both the generic mechanisms of global China – patron-clientelism, economic statecraft, and symbolic domination – as well as how they are deployed in Hong Kong. Unlike other target locations in the orbit of global China as a power project, Chinese sovereignty over Hong Kong lends Beijing unprecedented leverage while British colonial institutions have laid a strong foundation for Chinese internal colonization.

2.1.1 Hong Kong's Governance Crisis by Design

There is general consensus among scholars of Hong Kong that the Special Administrative Region (SAR) leadership failure in tackling a number of economic and public health problems since 1997 had sparked the half-million-strong July 1 protest in 2003 that raised the alarm in Beijing about Hong Kong as a rebellious territory and compelled it to take direct political control over the city. The sequence of incidents leading to this historic demonstration is indisputable: first the Asian financial crisis in the fall of 1997, then the bird flu outbreak at the end of that year; the chaotic opening of the new airport in 1998; followed by the SARS (severe acute respiratory syndrome) outbreak claiming the lives of 299 citizens and the government proposal to introduce a highly unpopular national security legislation in 2003. Through all these, the city registered a 66 percent plummet in residential real estate prices. Even though citizens from all walks of life were hard hit, the July 1, 2003, protest was driven significantly by the despair and anger of middle-class professionals, long the beneficiaries of Hong Kong's economic takeoff and the bedrock of regime support. Now the middle class found itself caught in negative equity, corporate retrenchment, and the threat of losing political freedom and civil liberties (Cheng 2005).

At the time, it certainly felt as if a curse had descended in the city since its handover to China, aggravated by the paternalistic style and sheer incompetence of the chief executive (CE), Tung Chee-hwa, originally a shipping tycoon. But beyond accidental external shocks and personality pitfalls, there were systemic weaknesses built into the SAR body politics that predetermined the occurrence and recurrence of governance crises. Wittingly or not, from the beginning, Beijing's political design for Hong Kong was to make the system accountable to itself rather than to the Hong Kong people. The Basic Law, imposed as the mini-constitution of the SAR, already prepared the way for Beijing's intervention, defeating its own blueprint of "One Country, Two Systems." First, the CE is elected by a Beijing-controlled Election Committee. In order to prevent the development of a local political base for the top official of the land, Beijing also prohibits the CE from having any party affiliation. Second, the Legislative Council, where business and professional elites are overly represented through a British colonial legacy institution called the "functional constituencies," is only partially returned by popular votes. The Legislative Council is further stymied by the constitutional stipulation that legislators cannot put forth private bills that entail public spending. The most they could do is to veto government's budget and bills (Ma 2007). In short, by design, there is no stable governing coalition at the top of an autocratic system that also lacks consent from a citizenry with increasing democratic aspirations.

The spark for the massive July 1, 2003, protest was Beijing's demand on the Hong Kong Government to enact a national security law (or "Article 23" in the Basic Law) that would curb civil liberties. Beijing's anxiety about national security in Hong Kong was in no small part due to Taiwan's transition of power from the nationalist Kuomingtang (KMT) to the independent-leaning Democratic Progress Party in 2000. Chinese officials began to see national security loopholes when, for instance, a convicted and deported Mainland Chinese dissident (Li Xiaomin) was able to find employment in a Hong Kong university, or when pro-independence politicians from Taiwan, including Vice President Annette Lu, were freely voicing their political ideology on a government-sponsored radio station. And, Falungong could legally and publicly operate as an organization in the city despite having been outlawed as an evil cult in the Mainland (Wong 2006).

With a mandate from Beijing, the ambitious careerist SAR Security Secretary Regina Ip decided to push the national security bill through, against widespread criticisms by the legal professions; journalists; students; religious, human rights, and civil society groups; and even chambers of commerce and bankers who were concerned about access to and disclosure of information (Petersen 2005). But when one-fifth of the population went to the streets to vent their anger at the government, even pro-establishment and pro-China politicians were pressured to distance themselves from the toxic situation. In September 2003, the chair of the Liberal Party, whose vote the CE needed to pass the bill, resigned in protest, while pro-Beijing politicians recommended withdrawal on pain of alienating their own electorate. Losing the support of the pro-establishment factions, the SAR government had no choice but to shelve the legislation, and stood humiliated by the resignations of Ip and Tung.

What the 2003 saga illustrated was not just the sovereign's imperative to impose its agenda on Hong Kong but also local officials' eagerness to cooperate with and exceed Beijing's expectations. Rather than taking a minimalist approach to enact Article 23, Hong Kong officials took an aggressive and expansive approach that went beyond its requirements in the Basic Law (e.g. giving police emergency power to search without warrant when investigating certain Article 23 offences and broadening the scope of "state secrets" and organizations to be prohibited). The spectacularly flawed manner in which officials conducted consultation was driven by arrogance and an inclination to show loyalty to their overlords, blinding them to sound political judgment about popular sentiment.

The Article 23 debacle also revealed a fundamental contradiction inherent in "One Country, Two Systems" blueprint – an authoritarian party-state and its careerist agents, ruling over a citizenry habituated to a common law tradition of legality and rights.

From the perspective of the Chinese government, the fact that Article 23 allows Hong Kong to enact its own laws governing offences like treason and theft of state secrets is already a concession, particularly since the responsibility for Hong Kong's defence lies with the Central People's Government. Yet, from the perspective of many Hong Kong residents, Article 23 is one of the greatest threats to civil liberties. Offences like "subversion" and "secession" are unknown in the Hong Kong legal system. (Petersen 2005: 1–2)

The stability of a political system with this contradictory and precarious coexistence of authoritarianism and liberalism at its core depends on restraint by the one country, and the acquiescence of the subordinate system. Since the early years of the SAR, these two conditions have rarely been obtained, and, in between them, is a group of political intermediaries whose career interests have fueled rather than mitigated conflicts. An enduring legitimacy crisis was therefore a foregone conclusion. As Scott (1989) explains, both popular consent and bureaucratic autonomy were in short supply due to the constitutional design of Hong Kong's political system and the imbalance of power between Hong Kong and China. No wonder then that, since 2003, as governance failure and popular resistance became a perennial and ubiquitous feature of the city's political life, the proclivity and determination for Central Government officials to intervene and to ensure control also heightened.

2.1.2 The Specter of Global Rebellions

Hong Kong's 2003 protest occurred amidst waves of mass rebellions in other world regions that magnified Beijing's concern for national security. As a matter of fact, since the collapse of the Soviet Union, there has been palpable fear among top Chinese communist leaders about the West's conspiracy of "peaceful evolution." The Color Revolutions in the Balkans in the early 2000s seemed to have confirmed their suspicions. Chinese pro-establishment academics explained these "contagious and illegitimate" political changes as being instigated by, among other things, "overt and covert interventions of Western powers, the United States in particular, that lent political and logistical support to the indigenous anti-authoritarian opposition" (Chen 2010: 7). When the Arab Spring protests took place in Tunisia and Egypt in 2010, high-level security efforts were put into effect nationwide in cyberspace and on the streets. The Ministry of Public Security urged the police to use micro blogs to "guide public opinion" and "pay attention to hot topics people are talking about on the Internet." Even more far-reaching was the creation of the State Internet Information Office, charged with centralizing the activities of a dozen government agencies, promoting "healthy development" in Chinese cyberspace, and monitoring and controlling social networking and gaming. An overwhelming show of police force in Beijing and other major cities was deployed to preempt rallies that in fact never materialized (Calabrese 2013).

The trope of "foreign interferences fomenting political instability" is routinely invoked to explain and justify Beijing's reactions to disturbance and separatism, ranging from the 2008 unrest in Tibet to the 2009 riots in Xinjiang, and Hong Kong's Umbrella Movement in 2014. After Xi Jinping's ascendance to power in 2013, the party-state took a hard-line approach to civil society. Whereas under the leadership of Hu Jintao and Wen Jiabao, the regime used a mix of protest bargaining, bureaucratic absorption, and grassroots patron-clientelism to maintain social stability through "social management" (Lee and Zhang 2013), Xi presided over a shift toward "prevention and control." Billed as a new national security theory with Chinese characteristics, and first proposed in 2014 and approved by the Politburo in early 2015, Xi's Comprehensive National Security Strategy calls for "a multi-dimensional information-based prevention and control system" to bolster eleven types of security: political, territorial, military, economic, cultural, social, science and technological, information, ecological, financial, and nuclear (Greitens 2021). Under the new strategy, external threats are refracted through the prism of how they will affect social stability and "political security" at home. Since 2013, the National People's Congress has passed or amended almost twenty pieces of security legislation that give the party-state enhanced power to deal with both internal and external challenges. The Hong Kong National Security Law that was passed in 2020 in response to the 2019 protests is just the latest of these, but others have tackled intelligence, counterterrorism, cybersecurity, and other cross-border and nontraditional threats. The media, Internet, universities, human rights lawyers, and feminists have all been subjected to the tightening grip of this securitization regime.

2.1.3 Exporting Surplus Capacity and Exalting Nationalism

Aside from governance and national security concerns, economic bottlenecks had spurred China to pursue global expansion since the late 1990s, engulfing Hong Kong along the way. Overcapacity, falling profits and market saturation threatened to stall growth, a foundation for the Communist regime's political legitimacy. Political economists of China have identified the systemic sources of overcapacity: local protectionism, fragmentation of industries, low input prices, weak enforcement of central government regulations, and a fiscal and cadre promotion system that encourages growth over profit. Anarchic competition among localities result(s) in uncoordinated construction of redundant productive capacity and infrastructure (Hung 2008). The problem was exacerbated by the 2008 global financial crisis, when the Chinese government rolled out a massive stimulus package that fueled even more debt-financed expansion of production capacity. A European Chamber of Commerce in China report finds precipitous decline between 2008 and 2014 in utilization rates of major industrial products including steel, aluminum, cement, chemicals, refining, flat glass, shipbuilding, and paper. Overcapacity implies falling profit and can lead to nonperforming loans, drain resources for technological upgrading, and heighten trade tensions with other countries. Chinese officials have been up-front about the need to export excess capacity to other developing countries through Going Out and the Belt and Road Initiative (BRI), framing these as a win-win solution for China and other countries. Going global also helps the government and businesses to expand the markets for Chinese goods and services, move up the value chain, and compete with other countries to set global norms and standards in technology (e.g. 5 G), international law (e.g. Seabed Laws), trade (e.g. e-commerce), and financing of infrastructure (e.g. Asian Infrastructure Investment Bank).

Beyond the central government, global China is driven by the interests of SOEs (state-owned enterprises), banks, ministries, and provincial and local governments. The BRI, like Going Out or Develop the West are not "carefully-worked out grand strategies" but typically platitudes, slogans, and catchphrases offering atmospheric guidance with which players can maneuver to serve their sectoral interests. Local governments, SOEs, and state banks lobbied hard to influence the translation of Xi's slogans into concrete policy in order to get part of the spoils (Jones and Zeng 2019). Huge government budgets were allocated to ministries core to the BRI. Besides the Ministries of Commerce and of Foreign Affairs, the Ministry of Culture, for instance, promotes BRI as a cultural exchange "brand," and cultivates cultural industry and trade along the BRI routes. Likewise, the Ministry of Education's 2016 action plan "commissions ten overseas science research institutions, and around five-hundred BRI think-tanks and research centers" (He 2019: 185). SOEs, tasked with exporting China's industrial goods and technology, are another beneficiary of global China. With state-provided bank guarantees, insurance, and subsidized working capital loans under Going Out to compete for international projects, China's international engineering and construction contracting industry is now a world leader, claiming some 25 percent of world total revenue and as much as 60 percent in Africa (Zhang 2020). These companies identify projects, secure financing from Chinese policy banks which conduct lending assessment and approve projects for governments to sign off on. Corporate profit motives of Chinese contractors drive these projects, relegating the host country's developmental prospect or debt sustainability to afterthoughts.

Going global resolves more than a potential crisis of overaccumulation; it also reinforces the legitimation and governance of Communist rule. Attaining global power and prestige allows the regime to fuel nationalism that buttresses CCP's autocratic rule. Official propaganda routinely invokes the refrain "hundred years of national humiliation," a reference to Chinese subjugation to Western encroachment in the pre-1949 era, to deflect foreign criticism of China's expansion abroad. In exalting the people to pursue "the Chinese dream of great national rejuvenation," Xi Jinping vowed to transform China into an economically, diplomatically, politically, socially, culturally, and militarily strong country (*qiangguo*): "Such a holistic approach calls for a focus on both internal and external security. Internally, it is essential to promote development, continue reform, maintain stability, and create a safe environment. Externally, we should promote international peace, seek cooperation and mutual benefit, and strive to bring harmony to the world" (China.org 2015). In the name of an all-inclusive range of "national security" responsibilities, he consolidated his power by creating the most centralized power structure within the party-state since Mao's times, setting up the National Security Commission in 2014 and dismantling the collective leadership system Deng Xiaoping put in place.

In a nutshell, Beijing's interventionist turn in Hong Kong was not just a reaction to the 2003 mass rally but was part of a protracted process of national securitization and global expansion that began in the wake of Hong Kong's retrocession. The Mainland regime was juggling the multiple imperatives of global economic integration, surviving the financial crisis originating in the West, and maintaining stability in the face of waves of popular unrest against autocracies. If the current reign of Xi Jinping is marked by a more aggressive push for global China (sometimes referred to as "wolf warrior" diplomacy named after a popular nationalistic Chinese film *Wolf Warrior*), coupled with heightened repressive control over domestic civil society than that by his predecessors, the reasons have to do with the mounting political economic pressures the regime perceives or projects in the post-2000 world, and not just his authoritarian personality and outsized political ambition.

2.2 Global Playbook, Local Application

Hong Kong is not just one of the many destinations of global China; it is actually global China's primary frontier, thanks to its established status as Asia's financial center and a global city. Built over 150 years, Hong Kong is China's most advanced international city boasting world-class legal institutions, professional expertise, banking and communication infrastructure, transregional and international business, and transportation networks (Chiu and Lui 2009). In particular, as a free financial and currency market at the doorstep of the Mainland where the financial market and currency are still not fully liberalized, Hong Kong serves an indispensable function to globalizing state-owned enterprises. It has become the most important window for Chinese enterprises to raise capital through initial public offerings (Hung 2018). Hong Kong offers Chinese public and private assets owners the opportunity to engage in "property rights arbitrage" (Naughton 1999). With its secure and transparent property rights regime, in close proximity to the vague and uncertain property rights regime in China, giant SOEs and officials find in Hong Kong a safe haven to park their public and private wealth, increase their operational autonomy, access information about the world market, and even take advantage of tax benefits due to their "foreign" registration in Hong Kong. Two sets of statistics show Hong Kong's essential frontline roles for China's outbound economic expansion. Hong Kong hosts most of Chinese companies' initial public offerings overseas (Figure 1) and is the major gateway for China's inbound and outbound foreign investments (Figure 2).

The dilemma for China is this: On the one hand, to serve its global expansion agenda, Hong Kong has to maintain its distinct institutions and way of life rooted in its common law legal system, free media, professional autonomy, and civil liberties. On the other hand, when signs of popular unrest surface, its sovereignty over Hong Kong also motivates and enables Beijing (and its many local agents) to exert a greater degree of control than is possible in other global destinations, even to the point of killing this proverbial goose that lays the golden eggs. With hindsight, we can see that during the first decade after 1997, when China considered it a paramount national interest to integrate with the global economy, its policy toward Hong Kong leaned toward tolerance and indirect control. However, as its global imperatives turn into conflicts and competitions with the West, as will be discussed later, securitization and direct control take priority.

Having explained the impetuses propelling China's global project, we now turn to how it is being pursued in Hong Kong. The three elements – patron clientelism, economic statecraft, and symbolic domination – in the global China playbook are familiar to scholars and citizens of China because they have been used within China. Yet, when these same modalities of power are used outside the Mainland and subjected to different configurations of local power dynamics, the consequences are often uneven and unintended.

2.2.1 Patron-Clientelism

At home and abroad, the CCP regime has a venerable tradition of skillfully cultivating social relations with people and communities to create patron-clientelism, or long-term relations of exchanging material and symbolic

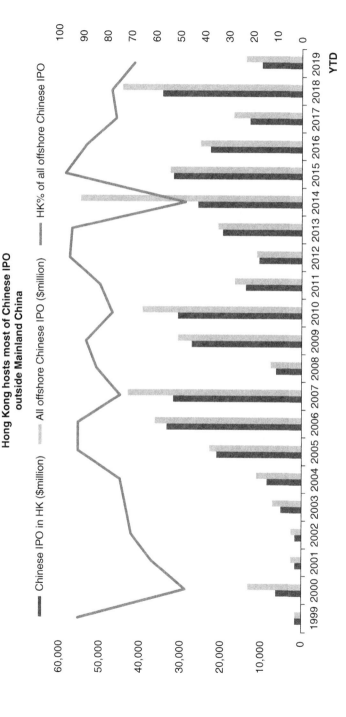

Figure 1 Hong Kong hosts most of Chinese companies' initial public offerings overseas.

Source: Reuters, September 4, 2019. www.reuters.com/article/us-hongkong-protests-markets-explainer-idUSKCN1VP35H

Global China

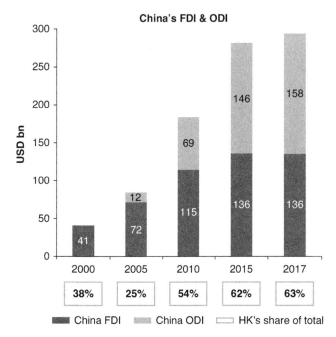

Figure 2 Hong Kong's share of China's foreign direct investment and outward direct investment.

Note: FDI occurs when a non-resident invests in the shares of a resident company. ODI occurs when a resident company invests in a wholly owned subsidiary or a joint venture in a non-resident country as part of a strategy to expand their business.

Source: Hong Kong Monetary Authority. www.hkma.gov.hk/eng/key-functions/inter national-financial-centre/hong-kong-as-an-international-financial-centre/dominant-gate way-to-china/

rewards for political support. Patron-clientelism has been well documented in CCP's governance of rural and urban China where the party-state leverages state control and selective distribution of life chances and economic, social, and political resources to forge unequal relations of dependence, loyalty, and support with citizens and cadres alike. One particular application of patron clientelism, originating in Lenin's revolutionary practice, is called the "united front." It targets opponents and non-CCP elements in order to neutralize their opposition or convert them into sympathizers.

As China goes global, the regime kindles expansive patron clientelist ties with foreign nationals, political elites, and the Chinese diaspora through its "united front" apparatus, an elaborate machine within the party-state. Its nine bureaus cover almost all of the areas in which the Communist party perceives threats to its power. The third bureau, for instance, is responsible for work in Hong Kong, Macau, and Taiwan, and among about 60 million overseas

Chinese in more than 180 countries. Under Xi Jinpiing, a leading group has been formed for united front work now with direct command from the Politburo. Its training manual (Kynge 2017) introduces a range of methods on how officials can use this "magic weapon," from emotional mobilization, stressing "flesh and blood" ties to the motherland, to ideological enticement to contribute to the "great rejuvenation of the Chinese people," and material rewards to selected overseas Chinese groups and individuals deemed valuable to Beijing's cause.

A US Congress report (Bowe 2018) and academic writings (Hamilton 2018, To 2014) document how the Chinese "united front" reaches far beyond the Chinese diasporic community, to include a broad range of sectors and players in Western societies. Politicians and members of parliament at federal and provincial levels in Australia, New Zealand, and Canada have been found to be "agents of influence" pushing for pro-Beijing policies, some even having direct connections to Chinese intelligence. Others are Chinese-born media moguls and influential community leaders who control the local Chinese-language media and promote pro-China narratives. Western critics assail this as "sharp power," a term popularized by a Hoover Institution report (Diamond and Schell 2019) to describe the opaque Chinese methods of "coercive, corrupting and corrosive" penetration. In the global south, Chinese foreign assistance projects are tools for building political patronage relations with political elites. For instance, a large-scale study on 1,650 Chinese development projects across some 3,000 physical locations in Africa from 2000 to 2012 found that political leaders' birth regions receive substantially larger financial flows from China in the years when they hold power compared to what the same region receives at other times. These biases are a consequence of electoral competition: Chinese aid disproportionately benefits politically privileged regions in country-years when incumbents face upcoming elections and when electoral competition is intense (Dreher et al. 2019).

At the community level, united front work uses financial incentives, logistical supports, and business opportunities to entice pro-China behavior among overseas clans associations, native place associations, Chinese business associations, councils for peaceful reunification of China, and the like. Economic incentives often come packaged with heavy doses of nationalistic rhetoric. The Chinese embassies, via their control over Chinese nationals' passport status and life chances of family members back home, can demand compliance of Chinese students and scholars abroad, eliciting their assistance in collecting information of foreign countries or forming crowds on the street to drown out anti-China protesters (To 2014).

In Hong Kong, Chinese patron-clientelism has reached unparalleled scope and depth, thanks to Chinese sovereignty. United front as a practical tactic and a bureaucratic apparatus has a long history in Hong Kong dating back to the 1920s, right after the founding of the CCP. Over the decades, taking advantage of the British colony's freedom and international connections, Communist cadres carried out united front work appealing for support in Hong Kong and overseas through newspaper and magazine publication, unions, schools, and recreation clubs, in addition to operating clinics, movie companies, and department stores. The penetration of united front work has gone so deep in Hong Kong that the "leftists" 左派, or "patriots" 愛國人士, constituted a self-sufficient community and economy that were in many ways an antidote and an alternative to Hong Kong's colonial, capitalistic and materialistic mainstream (Lui and Chiu 2014: 6–7). However, in the aftermath of the 1967 riots instigated by Hong Kong leftists during the Cultural Revolution years, which saw 51 deaths, 848 injuries and more than 7,000 bombs planted throughout the city, the appeal and influence of the left faded. United front work did not revive until the 1980s in preparation for Hong Kong's reunification with the Mainland.

During the transition to 1997, Beijing's salient priorities were to shore up local and international capitalists' confidence and keep democratization at bay, as massive capital outflow and popular mobilization would undermine not just Hong Kong's prosperity and stability but also China's economic development. The arrival in 1983 of the charismatic and liberal-minded Xu Jiatun as the new chief of the Xinhua News Agency, the local headquarters of united front work, marked the beginning of a new patron-clientelist dance between the capitalist class and the CCP that would later be continued by the Liaison Office of the Central Government in Hong Kong until today. As electoral politics grew in importance in the governance structure of Hong Kong, CCP's united front apparatus also grew its patron-clientelist networks at the grassroots among underprivileged social groups and community organizations. Their votes would then become the electoral bulwark for a new comprador class of pro-Beijing party politicians that the Liaison Office has groomed. How is Chinese elite co-optation different from the British colonial variety? What impact does it have on governance and protests?

China's co-optation of Hong Kong's business elite began before 1997, allowing them disproportionate influence in drafting the SAR's mini-constitution. Business tycoons were appointed to the various bodies responsible for administering the transition of sovereignty, including the Basic Law Drafting Committee, the Basic Law Consultative Committee, the Hong Kong Affairs Advisers, the Preliminary Working Committee, and the HKSAR Preparatory Committee. They also accounted for the majority of appointed representatives among Hong Kong's compatriots to the National People's Congress (NPC) and the National Committee of the Chinese People's

Political Consultative Conference (CPPCC). Honorific titles like these are vessels of scarce symbolic and social capital for the Hong Kong elite, allowing them privileged access to Mainland provincial and local officials who wield wide regulatory and approval powers in dealing with foreign capital.

The key difference between British colonial and Chinese co-optation is that, before 1997, the co-opted business elite did not have any institutionalized access to or share political economic agenda with the sovereign state in London. The colonial governor was the dominant party in the state–business alliance, and was able to transform the economic doctrine of laissez faire into a powerful ideological weapon and a governance ethics limiting elite claims on state resources. The alliance guaranteed a pro-business environment of low taxation and free competition, but no state assistance. Laissez-faire "was the basis of a social compact made necessary by the absence of democracy . . . The colonial administration created a clear distinction in Hong Kong political life between 'public' and 'private' interests" (Goodstadt 2009: 120–121). All this changed after 1997, when Beijing, rather than the chief executive becomes the de facto power center of the state–business alliance, and local capitalists are able to use their privileged access to the sovereign state to challenge the governing authority of the chief executive and to bargain for policy concessions. Such circumvention activities by the elite in key social policies such as housing, infrastructure development projects, and business regulations have eroded the SAR government's authority, autonomy, and legitimacy (Fong 2014).

Another very important difference between the state–business alliance under British and Chinese rules has to do with the changing nature and interests of the capital class. There was more inter-connectedness (measured by interlocked directorship) among the dominant British hongs, each with a diverse portfolio of business covering finance, transportation, retail, and real estate. As they retreated or fell into Chinese hands, the Chinese family business conglomerates grew without creating interfamilial alliances. As deregulation broke down old monopolies in telecommunication and transport, for instance, the economic power structure had become decentered, nucleated, and fragmented. Inter-group competition in the marketplace also spilled over to their rent-seeking lobby for preferential government policies and subsidized lands (Liu and Chui 2007). Private interests spoiled the neutrality of the state, which became the target of blame by businesses and the public alike. Finally, as local capital and mainland capital increasingly merged to form symbiotic relationships, and as business elites began to wear multiple hats as business and political leaders in both Hong Kong and China, capitalists' interest have gone beyond mere profit-making. The boundary of capitalist class politics became fussy – their politics extending beyond assuming formal positions in political institutions to include forming civic associations, setting up think tanks, and owning mass media (Ngo 2019). The scope of power wielded by the autocratic elite has therefore expanded.

Patron-clientelism is also used to entice the political support of the business and professional sectors, mainly in the form of functional constituency (FC) representation in the Legislative Council. Created by the outgoing colonial regime to increase its legitimacy in its final years and later on embraced by the new sovereign in Beijing, the franchise for FC election is reserved for members of major business and professional groups – chambers of commerce, industry associations, registered professionals, and social organizations such as unions, and cultural or sports groups. From 1998 to 2012, thirty seats, or half of the legislature, was elected by FCs, with the other half popularly elected after 2004. As most corporate voters are commercial corporations, which are seldom run democratically, FC has largely become a system representing sectoral leaders and corporation bosses. Not only that, FC sectors also account for almost 80 percent of votes in the election committee for choosing the chief executive. As a result, the post-1997 corporatist state had diverted a lot of resources and policy actions to selected sectors. When some sectors accused the government of favoritism – of offering particularistic benefits and subsidies to selected enterprises or sectors – the government invariably responded by dishing out new subsidies or policy actions to the complaining sectors or groups to pacify them. "Sectors put forth their particularistic demands as no overarching business coalition is capable of controlling the post-1997 Hong Kong state to embark on a unified strategy of development" (Ma 2016: 263).

At the grassroots, patron-clientelist united front work has been given a strong organizational, material, and ideological boost in the aftermath of the 2003 anti-government rally. The Liaison Office, tasked to create a second governance ladder in Hong Kong and to change hearts and minds of the Hong Kong people, has since expanded in size, personnel, and budget. "Mass organizations" – regional federations, hometown or clans associations, and service-oriented NGOs – and their affiliated organizations throughout the territory mushroomed. A typical example of grassroots co-optation was the Chaozhou hometown association. The Hungry Ghosts Festival was their traditional event and was losing popular appeal by the 1990s. Yet, the Chaozhou Community Organization and the Kowloon Federation of Associations have, since 2008, actively revived the event and spread it to more than a hundred neighborhoods. Such events were occasions to create grassroots clients among the elderly, working-class housewives, and new immigrants by distributing food, banquets, group tours, sports sponsorship, community facilities, human services, and even cash (Cheng 2020, Kwong 2009). The large number of united front organizations, loaded with human and financial resources, have penetrated the community, collecting addresses and phone numbers of their voter-clients. "Vote captains" would intensely track down their clients and make sure they turn out to vote during elections. The share of popular vote has increased steadily for the pro-Beijing camp. For District Board elections, from 2003 to 2015, the popular vote for pro-Beijing candidates increased from 52 percent to 76 percent. For Legislative Council election, it increased from 37 percent to 46 percent in 2016 (E. Lee 2020: 769–770). Beyond elections, these grassroots constituencies formed the backbone of pro-government mobilizations staged in opposition to pro-democracy rallies (Yuen 2021).

Among new immigrants from the Mainland – who now number about 60,000 annually under various schemes – the example of New Home Association is illustrative. Set up in 2010, it quickly expanded into an enormous organization with five district offices. By 2015, it claimed to have more than 100,000 members. Membership is free, but members receive numerous free gifts and benefits including food, concert tickets, discounted medical services, scholarships, and discounted tours and meals. In election times, new immigrants would be mobilized to vote when they participate in career development activities or "soft" social networking activities such as boat cruises, sports, or wine-tasting (Wong, Ma, and Lam 2018: 91).

In short, as the sovereign state, Beijing holds the ultimate power to distribute political and economic reward and punishment to facilitate its rule at both the elite and grassroots levels. United front work has markedly increased in scope, intensity, systematicity, and visibility in the past two decades, so much so that its command center, the Liaison Office, flanked by its vast network of affiliated elite and community associations, is being widely considered a "quasi-ruling party" (E. Lee 2020). Wielding king-making power, the Liaison Office has no qualm undermining the legitimacy, authority, and autonomy of the SAR government that is now even more beholden and accountable to Beijing than to the Hong Kong populace. Together with the Central Government's decisions in the years since 2003 to stall political reform toward full-scale democracy and universal suffrage, many in Hong Kong felt politically disenfranchised.

2.2.2 Economic Statecraft

Like many other countries, China deploys economic statecraft, or the use of economic relations and policy tools (including sanctions, taxation, embargoes, trade agreements, asset freezing, currency manipulation, subsidies, and tariffs) to pursue national interests in the international arena. What China calls "economic diplomacy" can be undertaken by state or private entities, because formal

ownership categories belie the intertwined and blurred boundaries of private
and state interests and control in China (Norris 2016). Concessional loans for
infrastructure construction, building artificial islands as territorial state-making,
and creating economic dependence through trade agreements are salient practices of Chinese economic statecraft that have been applied to different parts of
the world, including Hong Kong.

Since the export of surplus capacity is a primary goal of going global,
Chinese SOEs, especially those in infrastructure construction, have been the
frontline soldiers of state campaigns from Going Out to the Belt and Road
Initiative. The practice of extending Chinese state credits to developing countries to build infrastructure by Chinese state contractors in the name of development assistance was first applied to peripheral and restive minorities regions
within China. The Chinese government uses large-scale infrastructure projects
as a spatial fix for Chinese capital flow and consolidation of state power. Loans
are actually fiscal transfers to SOEs masked as development aid to provincial
governments in impoverished areas such as Tibet or Mongolia, embellished in
a "win-win" discourse of "mutual benefits." "Since 2013, a number of infrastructural projects built under the name of Going West, such as the Qinghai-
Tibet Railway, are now being extended beyond China's borders under the label
of the One Belt One Road Initiative, bringing together China's westward and
outward strategies" (Yeh and Wharton 2016: 291).

As part of this trend of exporting surplus capacity by China, post-1997
Hong Kong is the site of several multibillion-dollar infrastructural megapro-
jects. The high-speed railway connecting downtown Kowloon with China's
national high-speed rail system is a prime example of territorial state building
and dumping of excess capacity on Hong Kong where there is already ample
transportation connection with the Mainland. The twenty-six-kilometer high-
speed rail has the notorious distinction of being the world's most expensive rail
per kilometer, at a hefty cost of US$12 billion, and entailing a 30 percent budget
overrun. Despite widespread criticisms by pro-democratic politicians and the
public at large, the pro-establishment majority in the legislature had always
approved its ballooned financing. Most of the contracts were awarded to
Chinese state-owned contractors now dominant in the Hong Kong market
which used to see more international firms from Japan, Britain, and elsewhere.
In addition to allowing its SOEs to reap huge profits from the project, and
advancing the Mainland–Hong Kong border to the heart of the city from the
northern border areas in the New Territories, China has imposed an unprecedented "colocation" arrangement for custom clearance. One part of the massive
terminus is leased by Hong Kong authorities to their mainland counterparts to
allow passengers to pass through both immigration portals in one station.

It is where Chinese jurisdiction begins and where Hong Kong laws no longer apply, in clear violation of Article 18 of the Basic Law which stipulates that domestic Chinese law will not apply to Hong Kong. Colocation is tantamount to a zone of extraterritoriality reminiscent of semi-colonial Shanghai or other treaty ports in the late Qing era. We will see in the next section how the construction of this high-speed rail project triggered a landmark protest movement which had lasting impacts on the political consciousness and repertoire of contention for a whole generation of activists and citizens.

Another white elephant that serves China's rather than Hong Kong's interests is the Hong Kong-Zhuhai-Macao (HKZM) Bridge. It was approved by the Chinese government in August 2003 when the Hong Kong economy was reeling from a SARS-induced recession, and official rhetoric played up Hong Kong's dependence on China for economic recovery. Touted by Beijing as a Chinese engineering feat, the HKZM Bridge is the world's longest (55 km), most expensive (US$ 20b) sea-crossing bridge and estimated to be the most underused (taking seventy-two years to break even, if ever). Of the project's lucrative contracts, 78 percent were awarded to Chinese SOEs, incurring a 50 percent budget overrun. Adding insult to injury, the project exacted a heavy human toll (19 deaths and more than 600 industrial injuries), and was plagued by scandals of falsified concrete compression tests, defective seawalls, and destruction of habitat for white dolphins. Like the high-speed railway, the bridge realizes political and economic interests for China. First, it symbolizes, in a literally "concrete" way, Hong Kong's integration into the "Greater Bay Area," a megaregion, previously known as the Pearl River Delta, and part of China's latest national development strategy. Second, the project is the testing ground and a demonstration unit for Chinese constructors seeking to set global engineering standards and to showcase them to potential customers around the world. Tellingly, the *People's Daily* celebrated the opening of the HKZM Bridge by boasting that "constructors of cross-sea steel bridges from Germany, Serbia and Norway have signed contracts with Chinese enterprises, hoping the latter to offer Chinese technologies and materials produced on the same production line of the HZMB ... more bridges would be built in accordance with Chinese standards around the world in the future" (Yang 2019).

It should be emphasized that Beijing's economic statecraft in Hong Kong was sometimes the result not of external imposition but local elite engineering. In the case of the HKZM Bridge, Gordon Wu of Hopewell Holding, a major infrastructure construction company in Hong Kong, came up with the idea for the bridge which was shelved by both Beijing and the Hong Kong government prior to 1997. But in the aftermath of the Asian financial crisis and the rise of Guangdong province as a competitive neighbor, Hong Kong's first Chief

Executive Tung Chee-hwa began rallying the support of the Central Government's National Development and Reform Commission to revive the plan. A design proposed by Hong Kong was selected among other alternatives submitted by Guangdong and Shenzhen in 2003 (Yang 2006).

Among China's legion of infrastructure constructions around the world, none has become more controversial than the building of artificial lands. In the past decade, new ports and islands were built by Chinese contractors – Khalifa Port in Abu Dabi, Colombo Port City in Sri Lanka, Paranaguá and Antonina in Brazil, Manila's City of Pearl and Davao Bay in the Phillipines, Chittagong in Bangladesh, Gwadar in Pakistan, Hambantota in Sri Lanka, Kyaupkyu in Myanmar, Malacca in Malaysia, Mombasa and Lamu in Kenya, among a total of forty-two ports in thirty-four countries as of 2018. The bedrock of this capacity is the dredging industry, which was declared a priority growth area in 2001 by the Chinese government. Massive state investment in the past twenty years in dredging capacity and technology has allowed Chinese SOEs to corner the world market of artificial island building and land manufacturing. One massive state-owned company, China Communications Construction Corporation (CCCC) and its subsidiaries, now commands a dominant position in terms of both total hopper dredger capacity and total installed power on cutter suction dredgers (Benecki 2017). Profits aside, artificial land making is widely seen as also a military move to expand China's maritime jurisdiction in international waters. In the South China Sea, over the span of just a few years, Chinese-operated dredgers created seven islands with 3,200 acres of new land, enabling China's military to install runways, radar arrays, and air defense batteries in waters claimed by neighboring states (Watkins 2015).

In Hong Kong, a mammoth land reclamation project has been proposed by Beijing and its local agents. "Lantau Tomorrow Vision" is a HK$624 billion-grand plan aims to build 1,700 hectares of artificial island, or equivalent to one-fifth of urban Kowloon. With a projected cost equivalent to three-quarters of the city's fiscal reserve, it has been touted as the ultimate solution to resolve Hong Kong's land and housing shortage. The project, ridiculed as a foolish act of "dumping money into the sea," has attracted wide opposition from the start. Many in Hong Kong questioned its astronomical and soaring costs, damages to marine life, and its sheer necessity. Civil society organizations proposed an alternative focusing on the systematic redevelopment of so-called brownfield sites in the New Territories, which are abandoned plots of agricultural or rural land used for industrial workshops. Public opinion leaders even suspected that Beijing simply wanted a new urban center for its own elite to replace the Central District on Hong Kong Island. Yet, with a legislature firmly controlled by the pro-establishment camp, a bill to conduct a feasibility study for Lantau reclamation was passed in December 2020.

Finally, trade and investment have a pivotal role in economic diplomacy. One classic study by Albert Hirschman depicts how German commercial policies were designed to establish, deepen, and exploit southeastern European states' asymmetric structural economic dependence on Germany before World War II. In *National Power and the Structure of Foreign Trade*, Hirschman (1945: 31) distinguished between supply effect and influence effect flowing from asymmetry of economic dependence. Both are characteristic of Hong Kong's trade relation with China. Supply effect happens when "the conditions which make the interruption of trade [a] much graver concern to its [the supplying country's] trading partners than itself": the supplying country can use this opportunity to promote its interests by either directly threatening to cut off or weaken supply, if importing countries do not comply with its demands. Since the 1960s, Hong Kong has been dependent on China for supplies of water and food. By the end of 2013, some 95 percent of live pigs, 100 percent of live cattle, 33 percent of live chickens, 100 percent of freshwater fish, 90 percent of vegetables and 70 percent or more of flour on the Hong Kong market had been supplied by the mainland (Cheung 2014). Run by monopolistic Chinese companies, the unit price of fresh water in Hong Kong is among the most expensive in the world, and the rising cost of food has led to public outcry that does not find any response from the SAR government (Goodstadt 2018: 174–175).

But it is Hirschman's notion of "influence effect" flowing from asymmetrical trade relations that is particularly insightful and relevant to the era of global China. The dependent state becomes politically influenced not because of external pressure, but because of voluntary adoption; not because of economic deprivation from sanctions or severed trade, but because of economic benefits that accrue from the trade relationship. Wu (2015, 2019) uses this concept to underscore the "China factor" in Taiwan politics. As Mainland China accounted, respectively, for 30 percent and 73 percent of Taiwan's total export and outbound investment, Beijing utilized economic integration to set up cross-strait networks and cultivate "local collaborators" who spoke on behalf of Chinese interests at critical junctures. In 2012, echelons of tycoons induced economic voters to reelect the pro-Beijing presidential candidate Ma Ying-jeou.

Across the Strait, in Hong Kong, economic dependence through trade was not so much orchestrated by Beijing as actively pursued by the Hong Kong business and political elite, through a trade agreement called Closer Economic Partnership Arrangement, or CEPA. Seeking both profits and influence effects, and in order to take advantage of "first-mover" status after China's entry into the

World Trade Organization (WTO), the Hong Kong General Chamber of Commerce led in proposing the establishment of a "free trade area" between Hong Kong and the Mainland as early as 2000. The CEPA Agreement, approved by Beijing in 2003 when the Hong Kong economy hit a nadir due to the Asian financial crisis and SARS, not only allowed products of Hong Kong origin into the Mainland without tariffs, it also accorded preferential treatment to twenty-seven key service sectors, taking effect approximately two years before China had to open up its economy in accordance with the WTO schedule. In 2007, after continued effort from the SAR government and the Association of Banks, Mainland financial institutions were allowed to issue Renminbi-denominated bonds in Hong Kong. Hong Kong banks could also acquire share in Mainland banks, further opening the door for Hong Kong banks to establish subbranches in Guangdong. Yet, in most professional service sectors, such as medical, law, and accounting, after more than a decade, rampant protectionism, discrimination, and obstructions by local officials meant that liberalization under CEPA existed on paper only (Goodstadt 2018: 170).

Other than big business, all four chief executives of the SAR have been keen on integrating Hong Kong's economy with the Mainland. Tung Chee-hua lobbied for CEPA, Donald Tsang for the inclusion of Hong Kong into China's national Five Year Plan, Leung Chun Ying for a super-connector role for Hong Kong in the Belt and Road Initiative, and Carrie Lam for Hong Kong's integration into the Greater Bay Area. Their zeal in subsuming Hong Kong's economy under the Chinese economy was stunning in light of warnings by three Chinese premiers (Zhu Rongji, Wen Jiabao, and Li Keqiang) that Hong Kong's economic system is and should be kept international and unique, complimentary to but not integrated with that in the Mainland (Goodstadt 2018: 162). The SAR's activist role in pushing for integration with China stands in stark contrast to the government suspicion in the pre-1997 era and immediate post-handover years. Economic integration of Hong Kong and Mainland have grown in tandem with the fortune and political influence of the pro-China business elite in Hong Kong politics, even though an asymmetrical structure has developed whereby the Hong Kong economy is severely dependent on the China market, compared to its previously more diverse and international composition.

In the face of these extravagant white-elephant projects and imposed economic integration, Hong Kongers were quite powerless because they had been duly approved by a legislature dominated by pro-China representatives. Citizens' discontents found expression outside the political system. For ordinary people, socioeconomic integration with the Mainland in the forms of tourism and immigration caused the most tangible disruptions to their daily lives, triggering politically explosive popular reactions. Between 2003 and

2007, again in the name of Mainland China assisting Hong Kong, an expansive individual tourism scheme was introduced to allow tens of millions of Mainland tourists to travel freely to Hong Kong, rather than through organized tour companies. In a decade, the number of individual tourists from China increased from less than a million to 47 million a year, far exceeding the carrying capacity of a city of 7 million. Birth tourism also flourished, as Mainland pregnant women attracted by Hong Kong's superior medical and educational facilities came to give birth, straining public resources for local mothers. The numbers of children of non–Hong Kong parenthood ballooned from less than 1,000 a year to more than 35,000 in 2011 (Ma 2015). Such an influx of Mainland citizens occurred on top of the "one-way permit" scheme which was put in place in 1980. Designed for spouses and dependent children of Hong Kong permanent residents, it allows a daily quota of 150 immigrants from the Mainland who have accounted for more than 90 percent of annual population growth in the past two decades. Mainland authorities have staunchly refused to share with Hong Kong its exclusive power over the selection and approval of immigrant applications. In all, in addition to the 1 million new immigrants holding one-way permits, another 70,000 Mainlanders have come under the "Mainland Talents and Professionals" scheme that began in July 2003, presumably to resolve labor market shortage of skilled professionals.

These immigration streams have a profound impact on Hong Kong's political economic landscape. A survey of Mainland immigrants finds that they are economic migrants who tend to be more politically conservative and pro-establishment than Hong Kong natives. This gives credence to pan-democrats' suspicion that the Chinese government attempts to consolidate its rule by exporting emigrants to Hong Kong (Wong, Ma and Lam 2016). Beyond election, the job market has also overtime shifted in favor of Mainland workers as Mainland corporations became dominant in different sectors of the economy. For instance, by 2020, locals' share of investment banking jobs in the city has slumped to about 30 percent from 40 percent two years ago, with 60 percent of roles now filled by mainlanders and 10 percent by overseas nationals (Chan 2020).

On a more experiential level, the influx of tens of millions of Mainland Chinese added a palpable pressure in the everyday life of Hong Kong residents, amounting to a colonization of their life worlds. Overcrowded subway trains and long lines for local residents going to work inconvenienced many. Shops catering to local residents' daily necessities went out of business and were replaced by jewelry stores and factory outlets of luxury brands. Pharmacies stocked their shelves with infant milk powder purchased in bulk by Mainland tourists rather than regular over-the-counter medications needed by locals.

Verbal and physical skirmishes in public places between local residents' and Mainland visitors over norms of civility, mannerisms, and sanitation became common. Some of these episodes were recorded by smart phones and went viral, triggering sensational and inflammatory comments about invasion by "yellow locusts." Outraged residents in the New Territories even staged "reclamation action day" protests against suitcase-bearing tourists seemingly engaged in parallel border trade. All of these would inadvertently spark a momentous and fateful localist political movement that would change the course of Hong Kong forever.

2.2.3 Symbolic Domination

A third form of power in the global China playbook is what Pierre Bourdieu terms "symbolic domination." Emphatically distinct from "ideology," symbolic domination refers to the production and reproduction of power through symbolic forms (e.g. media, language, art, religion) with their ability to construct, name, and classify realities, to make certain things thinkable, even natural. Symbolic power has a magical quality achieved through mobilizing people's dispositions, feelings, common sense, and construction of reality (Bourdieu 1991; Bourdieu and Wacquant 1992). As with economic statecraft and patron-clientelism, symbolic domination has long been a Communist power strategy in governing the Chinese mainland and is now being exported abroad. While Beijing cannot achieve the same level of control over school curricula, the publishing industry, and mass and social media or instill patriotism in other sovereign states, the top leadership is keenly aware of the importance of symbolic power in advancing its global agenda.

In 2007, then-President Hu Jintao included culture as a factor of "comprehensive national power" and began programs to burnish China's "soft power." In recent years, Xi Jinping spoke about seizing discursive power internationally, "telling a good China story," "spreading China's voice well," and creating a "credible, loveable and respectable" image of China. Chinese media and think tanks have coined buzz words such as "China Model," "Peaceful Rise," and "China Dream" to counter Western discourses of "China Threat," "Chinese neo-colonialism" and "China's Collapse" (Callahan 2015). Among elite intellectuals, a group of "statist" thinkers have developed theoretical arguments for Chinese exceptionalism and rejection of Western liberalism and universal values. Drawing inspiration from Carl Schmitt, the authoritarian German legal and political theorist known for his affiliation with the Nazi regime, these public intellectuals have created a "new Schmittism." The theory justifies the supremacy of "sovereignty" over the rule of law and affirms the Party's leading role vis-a-vis the constitution, Chinese sovereignty in cyberspace, national security, territorial and social control, and the constituting power of the Party as the direct representative of the people (Veg 2019: 39). A related but global-level idea was the "China solution" 中国方案 which was announced by Xi at CCP's ninety-fifth anniversary in 2016. Refuting Francis Fukuyama's famous "End of History" thesis, Xi proclaimed that "History never ended ... nor can it ... The Chinese Communist Party and the Chinese people are fully confident that they can provide a China Solution to humanity's search for better social institutions." The China solution offers Chinese public goods and capital to address global threats – rising protectionism, wealth gaps, environmental damage, and unregulated cyberspace (Kelly 2017).

In the mass media, the rebranding of China Central Television as China Global Television Network (CGTV) is a multibillion-dollar effort to produce and disseminate state-sanctioned perspective on global news, allowing China to compete directly with other news agencies like Reuters, Bloomberg, CNN, and the BBC. Currently, CGTV broadcasts six channels, two in English and others in Arabic, French, Russian, and Spanish, with reporting teams in more than seventy countries. In radio broadcasting and the print media, China has either bought stakes in existing outlets, used front companies to mask its editorial control, or established its own networks of publication and distribution from Africa to America.

In Hong Kong, Beijing's attempts at symbolic domination follow the general template for global China but go deeper. Beyond symbols of sovereignty – the People's Republic of China (PRC) national flag ubiquitously displayed throughout the city, and the national anthem and a propaganda video made part of the daily broadcast on Hong Kong's Chinese-language television stations every evening since 2004 – Beijing targets particularly the media and basic education curricula. And as in government and politics, China repurposes tools of power adopted by the British colonial regime. Foremost among these is the co-optation of media owners and major shareholders by awarding them symbolic capital in the form of honorific titles (Ma 2007, Lee 2018). Since the 1990s, business elites saw media ownership as a wise political investment for their China portfolios. Notable examples include the acquisition of the *South China Morning Post* by Robert Kuok and then by Jack Ma of Alibaba, *Ming Pao* by Malaysian tycoon Tiong Hiew King, and the now defunct Asia Television Ltd. by Mainland Chinese businessman Wong Ching and others. As one media scholar notes, the concentration of media into the hands of not a single corporation, but a group of business people sharing the same basic interest in appeasing the Chinese government undermines the political plurality that existed in the colonial era (Lee 2018).

The transformation of Hong Kong's first and dominant free-to-air broadcaster TVB into a local equivalent of the Mainland official mouthpiece CCTV is the most dramatic illustration of Beijing's attempt at symbolic domination. Nicknamed "CCTVB" for its pro-Beijing news contents and editorial orientations, TVB has for decades had a ubiquitous presence in millions of homes, restaurants, and public places. Even in a digital age, it is the default channel for news among the elderly and the working class, and in a unique position to induce habitual submission and disposition to a particular construction of reality. Since 2015, TVB has been under the control of Li Ruigang, a media mogul nicknamed "China's Rupert Murdock" and one-time senior Communist Party official in Shanghai with an entrepreneurial mindset (Chen 2017). A long-time journalist at TVB (Au 2017) details how censorship operated as an invisible cage, realized through structurally embedded rules and the constitution of norms in the news department. Owners appoint managers who convey value judgment about current events to frontline journalists, mark the boundaries of legitimate and illegitimate controversies, allocate air time unevenly among political groups, and select images and interviews advantageous to one party over another, all resulting in a pro-establishment construction of reality.

In publishing, the Liaison Office's wholly owned Guangdong Xin Wenhua owns at least thirty publishing houses and brands, one of the biggest commercial printing companies in greater China, and sixty retail bookstores in Hong Kong and Macao. It publishes school textbooks, runs an online news outlet with almost 250,000 Facebook followers, and distributes pro-Beijing magazines to more than 500 secondary schools in Hong Kong. Sino-United, a Liaison Office's subsidiary company, has an outsized presence in the city's publishing industry, recording annual revenue of about HK$ 4 billion (US$516 million), or 80 percent of Hong Kong's HK$ 5 billion total book sales. With such "a wide spectrum of control over the market of knowledge distribution," as one independent book store owner observed, the Liaison Office effectively blocks the dissemination of books and authors it deems objectionable or subversive (Schmidt 2020).

Another realm of symbolic domination is the school system. The politics of curriculum reform and the high school subject of "national" education have provoked some of the most extraordinary popular mobilizations in post-1997 Hong Kong. Whereas school curriculum in the colonial era sought to cultivate a stateless, apolitical and anti-Communist, ethno-cultural Chinese identity among local students, the SAR government has been under mounting pressure from Beijing and pro-Beijing forces (such as pro-PRC schools and teachers associations, and PRC's satellite organizations and supporters, most notably delegates of NPC and CPPCC) to implement "national" and "nationalistic" education (Lau, Tse, and Leung 2016). In the first decade after 1997, official strategies for raising national consciousness entailed mainly nonmandatory extracurricular activities – museum visits, military youth camps, Chinese calligraphy, and folk dancing classes. Financial support to schools and NGOs offering national education activities was provided under various subsidy schemes. Even when a general reform of the school curriculum identified "moral and civic education" as a curricular area in 2000, the SAR government took a soft approach to "national identity," and "emphasized personal morality, portraying identity as a multi-level concept extending to notions of global citizenship" (Tse 2007). But after President Hu Jintao in 2007 (on the tenth anniversary of the SAR) explicitly emphasized the need for national education, and surveys consistently showed young people's strong identification as either Hong Kong people or Hong Kong Chinese rather than Chinese (Morris and Vickers 2015), the SAR government was compelled to act. In May 2011, the Education Bureau (EDB) released a consultation paper on making "Moral and National Education" a mandatory subject from 2012 or soon thereafter.

Parents and professional teachers' groups objected to the "brainwashing" and "spoon-fed patriotism" contents of the textbooks for national education. In these texts, China's Communist government is described as a progressive and selfless regime upholding stability and prosperity; multiparty democracy in the West is dismissed as a chaotic, conflict-ridden system that victimizes ordinary citizens; and controversial episodes such as the 1989 Student Movement (and the associated Tiananmen Massacre) were ignored. Social opposition quickly mushroomed to encompass a broad coalition of over twenty civic groups comprising the main teachers' union, religious bodies, parents and, not least, "Scholarism," a high school student group led by fourteen-year-old Joshua Wong. After months of massive protests and a hunger strike, the SAR government was forced to concede: moral and national education would be optional, not compulsory.

Resistance against Beijing's self-professed project of "winning the hearts and minds" of the Hong Kong populace seemed widespread and persistent, especially among the younger generation. Poll results on people's self-identification as "Hong Kongers" or "Chinese" show a colossal failure on the part of Beijing (Figure 3 and 4). Among people in the eighteen to twenty-nine age group, those claiming a "Hong Konger" identity has grown from 42 percent 1997 to 80 percent in 2020. A poll in June 2019 found that Hong Kong people's sense of pride in becoming a national citizen of China has plunged to 27 percent, while the percentage of those not feeling proud surged to 71 percent, registering all-time record low and record high since 1997, respectively. As for people's appraisal of the Central Government's policies on Hong Kong, all figures have turned

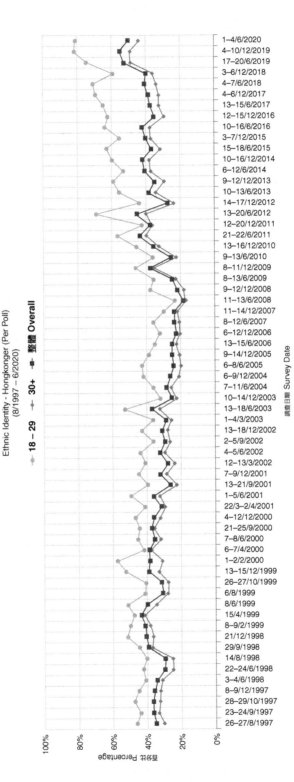

Figure 3 Hong Kong residents identifying themselves as "Hong Kongers" and not Chinese or Hong Kong Chinese
Source: Hong Kong Public Opinion Research Institute (PORI). www.pori.hk/pop-poll/ethnic-identity/q001/hongkonger

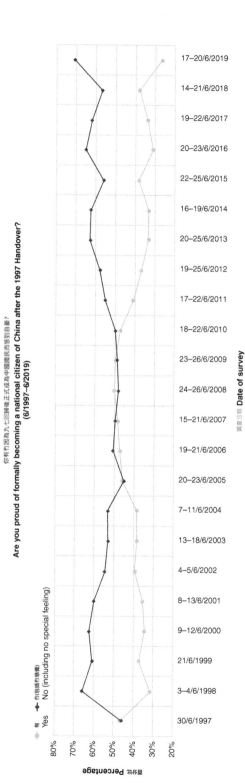

Figure 4 Decline in popular identification with China

Source: Public Opinion Program, University of Hong Kong. www.hkupop.hku.hk/english/popexpress/handover/ethnic/handover_ethnic_chart

negative. The latest proportion of positive appraisal stands at 23 percent, negative appraisal at 53 percent, resulting in a net value of negative 30 percentage points, which is an all-time record low since 1999. In-depth analyses show that the younger the respondents, the less likely they are to feel proud of becoming a national citizen of China, and also the more negative they are toward the Central Government's policies on Hong Kong (Public Opinion Program 2019).

2.3 Conclusion: Fractures and Discontents

In 1997, Hong Kong was returned to a China, which was not just Communist but also globalizing. What has happened in the global city since has stemmed from the agendas and practices of a globalizing Communist regime. The foregoing discussion has shown that the phenomenon of global China entails multiple power mechanisms and agents. Like other forms of globalization, be it neoliberalism or transnational civil activism, global China is a project that seeks embeddedness (Polanyi 1944) in local society, and inevitably opens up political spaces for countermovements, introducing new fractures and discontents.

In Hong Kong, Chinese power through patron-clientelism, economic statecraft, and symbolic domination grafts onto local institutions (e.g. executive-led political system, co-optation of business elite, native-place associations, schools, and newsrooms). Many among the Hong Kong political and economic elite have acquiesced and adapted to the shift in the wind, some even eager to exceed the expectations of their Beijing overlords in carrying out their biddings (e.g. national security legislation, infrastructure projects, media takeover, and curriculum reform). Others appropriate Chinese intervention to reap windfall profits and political capital. Even at the grassroots, and among the elderly, new immigrants, and working-class communities, patron-clientelism has bolstered popular support for the pro-Beijing establishment camp.

Yet, at the same time, there are limitations to what China can achieve. Disgruntlement and alienation brewed among opposition politicians, activists in civil society, the large and cosmopolitan middle class, and the well-educated younger generations. To them, the malaise of post-1997 Hong Kong – political disenfranchisement, economic subsumption, and colonization of their everyday life world – was caused by Beijing's interventions. As we shall see next, their successive collective mobilizations against Chinese encroachments constituted – for the first time in Hong Kong's history – a momentous decolonization movement from below. With hind sight, the July 1, 2003, mass demonstration turned out to be just the opening salvo of a two-decade-long struggle to regain citizens' birthright to the global city.

3 Countermovement: Decolonization from Below

As a free port and Asia's transportation hub, Hong Kong has long been famed for its bustling commerce and glistering malls, with an unabashedly ostentatious materialistic ethos to boot. Its rise first as a regional and then global financial center since the late 1970s attracted multinational corporations eager to trade with China and a transnational professional class enticed by its world-class amenities and luxuries. A so-called shoppers' and capitalists' paradise, the city has been the iconic face of capitalism that, as Marx put it most memorably, "presents itself as 'an immense accumulation of commodities.'" Marx (1992 [1867]: 125) Yet, against the grain, since Hong Kong formally became a semi-autonomous region within the world's largest Communist regime, it had acquired a new distinction as a "city of protests" (*Washington* Post 2000; see Figure 5). How did this counterintuitive metamorphosis happen?

Reviewing the major protests in the past two decades (Figure 6) reveals that China's interventions were the main, but not the only, triggers of popular resistance. Hong Kong citizens also campaigned against neoliberal capitalist tendencies wreaking havoc elsewhere in the world. True to its global city status, post-1997 Hong Kong was home to social justice movements reacting against the privatization of public goods and government services, public–private partnerships, casualization of labor, socioeconomic polarization, income inequality, and unaffordable housing. Against the government's prevailing narrative of developing Hong Kong as "Asia's world city," middle-class professionals, environmental NGOs, students, and unions pushed back, making claims of "right to the city," accountability, participatory planning, quality of life, worker rights, and grassroots livelihoods. It must be emphasized that these anti-neoliberalism protests were rather tame and mild episodes of collective action that mostly entailed writing petitions to the government or small-scale protests. For instance, the 2011 Occupy Central campaign activists, who pitched their tents under the Hong Kong Shanghai Bank Building in solidarity with Occupy Wall Street in the United States, attracted only a few dozen people on average throughout the seven months of their protest. The forty-day dockworkers' strike, which garnered significant public support and concessions from the employer, was a singular success. Its momentum dissipated at strike's end without an enduring impact on the local labor movement. The contribution of these social-economic protests lied mainly in nurturing a repertoire of action, rather than in challenging Hong Kongers' widespread acceptance of the liberal creed, market rationality, and the privatization of economic trouble. The objective realities of economic inequality seldom fueled impactful and mass mobilization.

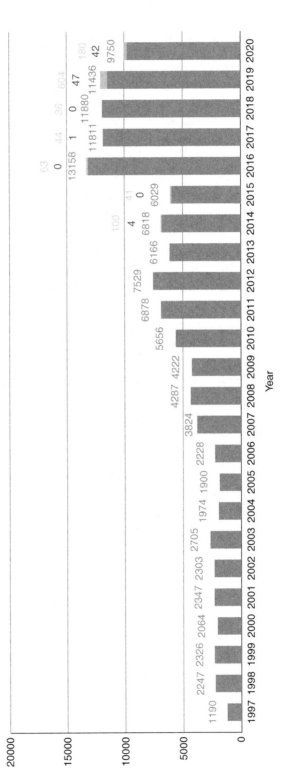

Figure 5 Rising volumes of protests
Source: Hong Kong Legislative Council Meeting Minutes, various years

1998–99	Controversy on Right of Abode
2003	July 1st Rally against Article 23 legislation

2003–4	Campaigns against harbor reclamation
	    Privatization of public housing assets (Listing of The Link
	    REIT) West Kowloon Cultural Hub development

11–18 Dec. 2005	Anti-WTO
Nov.–Dec. 2006	Preserving Star Ferry Pier
Jan.–July 2007	Preserving Queen's Pier
2003–8	Preserving Lee Tung Street
Nov. 2009–Jan. 2010	Anti-express railway link, protect Tsoi Yuen Village
2011–12	Occupy Central (spin off of Occupy Wall Street)
July–Oct. 2012	Anti-national education campaign
2012–19	Restoration Actions in border towns (anti-parallel trade)
Mar.–May 2013	Dockworkers' strike
Mar. 2013–Sep. 2014	Occupy Central with Love and Peace
Oct. 2013	Reissuing free-to-air television licenses
June 2014	Campaign against North-East Development Plan
Sep.–Dec. 2014	Umbrella Movement
8–9 Feb. 2016	MongKok Riot
2017–18	Campaign against colocation arrangement at West Kowloon Express Rail Terminal
2019–20	Anti-extradition protests

Figure 6 Major Protests and Events after 1997

3.1 Return of the Repressed

The most powerful and consequential protests were those reacting to Chinese domination and not neoliberal capitalism. In this sense, the Hong Kong chronicle of resistance amounts to a fight for decolonization, albeit one that had been delayed, denied, and repressed. Hong Kong did not partake in the decolonization process that swept across the globe in the post–World War II era, thanks to the strategic interests of both Britain and China to keep its colonial status. Yet decolonization – understood as a broad struggle to liberate the natives from external domination in politics, economics, culture, and the mind – has returned with a vengeance in the post-1997 era. From small-scale campaigns with modest, piecemeal goals – such as defending civil rights, preserving the harbor and historical architecture, rejecting political indoctrination in textbooks, demanding electoral reforms and repeal of draconian legislations – the struggle grew to a society-wide rebellion with some clamoring for independence in 2019. If China's interventions explain people's discontents and motivation for protests, what explains Hong Kong society's capacity to mobilize in massive numbers, especially given China's sovereignty and structural domination?

3.2 Events and Political Generations

As discussed previously, "events" are a rare subclass of happenings that, instead of being produced by structure, have the potential to significantly disrupt structure. Structures are sets of cultural schemas, distributions of resources, and modes of power combined in an interlocking and mutually sustaining fashion to reproduce consistent streams of social practices. As "concentrated moments of political and cultural creativity," events have the effect of "constituting and empowering new groups of actors or by re-empowering existing groups in new ways," putting in motion social processes that are "inherently contingent, discontinuous and open ended" (Sewell 2005: 110).

Among the many protests in the post-handover era, those that have "eventful" effects include: the July 1st rally (2003); the Star Ferry Pier, Queen's Pier, and Anti-Express Rail protests (2007–10); the anti-National Education Campaign (2012); the Umbrella Movement (2014); and the Anti-extradition Protests (2019). This section examines how the claims and strategies of Hong Kong's decolonization struggle emerged and evolved *through* these events over time. But first, I want to note the collective agency driving these events. After all, if contingency plays a big role in the sudden eruption of events transcending structural domination, it also augments the necessity and importance of agency.

My own research on leaders and activists in these movements points to the rise of a self-conscious post-1997 political generation spearheading these events. If a political generation is defined by shared "exposure to and participation in the social and intellectual symptoms of a process of dynamic destabilization" (Mannheim 1952: 30), an analysis of selective key figures in these events can illuminate the *collective* subjectivity and historicity that propel and are formed through events. Coming of age in post-1997 Hong Kong, these activists took postcoloniality more seriously than Beijing had intended, and created various self-identifications with reference to "generation." They called themselves the "post-80s generation," "post-90s generation," and "autonomous generation," or the "cursed generation." Yet, beneath these internal differentiations, they were all global, digital, and social media natives, in that global connections as well as digital and social media affordances were their natural habitats and survival skills. Through direct action in events, they accumulate a repertoire of strategy and develop a sense of empowered agency about their place in Hong Kong's history and future.

The activism trajectory of Eddie Chu, a key figure of the self-professed post-80s generation leading the Star Ferry, Queen's Pier, and anti-Express Rail protests, began with what he called a "natural interest in global developments." After graduating from college in 1999, he found himself surrounded by contemporaries who worked for international NGOs, including Green Peace, and he was so interested in global affairs that he went to Iran and Afghanistan to learn Persian and became a war correspondent for the Hong Kong press. Returning to Hong Kong, he witnessed protesters' "direct action" first hand during the anti-WTO protest in 2005 and became a key player among his fellow activists to turn the newly emerged independent internet-based media into a platform of activism.

> For our generation who experienced June 4 and July 1 mass rallies when we were primary school students, political participation is normal. When we started the Star Ferry preservation campaign, our brand of direct action was actually the composite of Greenpeace and Korean farmers. Greenpeace was part of the battle in Seattle and our friends working there had manuals about how to chain yourself to the ground, how to create dramatic social impact with a small number of people ... We could not adopt all the strategies of the Korean farmers, their militancy, like charging at the police with sharp objects. At that time, activists and the police in Hong Kong saw each other as opponents, not enemies to harm. Hong Kongers only adopted the Korean farmers' foreplay – ascetic walks, jumping into the sea, festive chanting and drums.[1]

Chu's personal account of taking up direct action for the first time vividly illustrates how an "event" can break the hold of power structure and transform agency. His globalism also morphed into localism by engaging in the practice of resistance.

> We always knew we were Hong Kongers. But that's our background only. Growing up under colonial rule, and knowing the Sino-British Declaration already set down the rules for our future, we always thought there was nothing we could do. But the moment I charged into the Star Ferry construction site and climbed up the excavator, I suddenly realized that was the first time I made a decision to resist, the first time I made a decision *for* Hong Kong. I could resist and stop something from happening ... Social movement activism is a process for me. I did not see a path or have any theory

---

[1] Interview with author, December 17, 2020.

beforehand. I wanted to be a global citizen, doing justice anywhere is fine. I went to Iran because I thought there was nothing to be done about Hong Kong's future. It's set. I now realize only a Hong Kong person, not any American, would charge into the Star Ferry site that day. Everyone has a unique role to play in local politics.[2]

Joshua Wong, born in 1996, first came to prominence as the founder of Scholarism in the 2012 anti-national education movement. He credited the 2009 anti-Express Rail protest led by Eddie Chu as his political enlightenment. Self-identified as part of the post-90s generation, Wong is a typical digital and social media native, and the 2012 campaign was the first mass movement in Hong Kong to ride the wave of the Facebook craze to mobilize more than 120,000 local protesters and garner global support. "Like any other Hong Kong teenager, I just played computer games. I learnt about politics online, following arguments among social activists on the internet and looking at how the different parties among the Pan-Democrats were failing to organize any effective opposition in the city. You could say Facebook was my library" (Wong 2015: 46). When the government yielded to the anti-national education protests, Wong and his fellow students at Scholarism wanted more. "Based on my experience, I was optimistic. We felt we had just won a big victory, and should be aiming for another. Not merely the right to vote directly for the Chief Executive, but also to choose who would be the candidates" (Wong 2015: 47). Although he admitted that he was not influenced by the Arab Spring, Occupy Wall Street, or 1989 Tiananmen Square protests, the global media sensation he created as the face of the Umbrella Movement in 2014 lent him disproportionate capability to internationalize the Hong Kong issue. Right after the Umbrella Movement, Wong opened an international frontline for Hong Kong's decolonization struggle by lobbying the US Congress to introduce a bill on the conditions of Hong Kong's human rights and democracy. This bill was finally passed at the height of the 2019 protests.

He reflected on how he and Hong Kong as a whole were inspired and empowered through events.

> It (the Umbrella Movement) greatly increased political awareness in Hong Kong society, as more and more people joined the movement. The city had no prior experience of large-scale civil disobedience. In 2012, the campaign against National Education involved no civil disobedience – at that time I myself was against it. The Umbrella Movement made it much more widely accepted as an instrument of change – in my view, as the only route to

---

[2] Interview with author, December 17, 2020.

change in the political system, after twenty years of futile agitation of a conventional sort. Of course, this time we gained nothing by way of political reform. The government refused to give way, and the movement eventually came to an end without achieving any of its aims. But we didn't lose the war, because we'll start the next round stronger than we did this one.

(Wong 2015: 49–50)

By the time of the 2019 anti-extradition movement, the narratives and vocabulary created during the Umbrella Movement became the disposition of the new cohort of protesters. When Chinese University Student Union president Au Cheuk Hei was sentenced to six months of imprisonment for unlawful assembly and possession of assault weapons in 2019, he addressed the court during his trial with a statement of defiance. The letter opened a window into the mind of this young rebel as well as many of what Au called "the generation of self-determination."

> The Occupy protest platform demanded that we determine our own fate 命運自決. That made a deep impression on me ... Tears and sweat mixed together, and seeing through the mist, an answer to my childhood question was slowly and hesitantly emerging: the greatest value to life is to decide your own fate [as autonomy/self-determination] ... Due to historical reasons, our generation does not have the power to choose not to live in a Hong Kong where the space for free speech and political rights has been decimated. Two summers back (i.e. 2019), we chose to reject our predetermined fate. We showed the world our autonomous consciousness. Now we have to accept responsibility for our choice ... Whatever awaits me in the future, I believe we are forever the generation of self-determination: we are using different ways to do our parts to create a new and fine era that belongs to us.[3]

Au's contemporary, Prince Wong, who was arrested for participating in a primary election and unlawful assembly, echoed, "It's the fate of our generation. We were just born in a period of historical political change. This is something we have to face."[4]

These sample snapshots indicate the power of action and events to shape new visions and political agencies that accumulate and resonate among contemporaries experiencing the same epochal structural forces. Using events and political generations as analytical drivers, we can now retrace how the claims and tactics of Hong Kong's decolonization struggle have evolved in the post-1997 period. The outbreak of the historic 2019 anti-extradition movement was both a culmination and a breakthrough of this two-decade-long trajectory.

---

[3]   Au, C. H. (2021). Self statement to Magistrate Ip Kai-leung at Kowloon City Magistrates' Courts, May 18. This translated version appeared online but is no longer available.

[4]   www.reuters.com/article/uk-hongkong-democracy-activists-special-idINKBN28A1GK

3.3 First Ruptures

An event begins with a rupture – a break with routine practice that triggers a sequence of interrelated ruptures, disarticulates the previous structural network, makes repair difficult, and makes a novel rearticulation possible (Sewell 1996). The eruption of three protests marked the initial ruptures in Hong Kong's popular political experience. The 1967 riots instigated by local Communists, the May 1989 demonstrations to support the Tiananmen students, and the July 1st rally in 2003 opposing the SAR government's national security legislation share the same "other" – the Communist Mainland perceived as a land of violence, chaos, lawlessness, and tyranny – against which Hong Kongers defined themselves as a separate political community. These were historic moments of popular awakening when people were compelled to ask the collective existential question: Who are we as a people, as Hong Kongers? For them, the answer lies in the core values of nonviolence, rule of law, and civil liberty that undergird their lives in Hong Kong.

During the summer of 1967, Communist sympathizers in Hong Kong, emboldened by the rebellious Red Guards of the Cultural Revolution on the Mainland and hailing the banner of anti-colonialism, resorted to violence by planting a thousand bombs throughout the city. Literally shell shocked, and reeling from innocent deaths of children and public figures alike, local residents, including the historian Elizabeth Sinn who experienced the riot personally, had an epiphany.

> Before the riot, even though Hong Kongers felt some distance from the Mainland, no one mentioned the term "Hong Konger." No one asked questions like "who am I." But during the riot, this question became an awakening. People were forced to choose between being Hong Konger and being Chinese, or Chinese under Communist rule. Therefore, in 1967, there was a salient transformation from being Hong Kong residents to Hong Konger.
>
> (quoted in Tsui 2017 199–200)

Public opinion was overwhelmingly in favor of the colonial government's high-handed arrests, imprisonment, and deportation of more than a thousand rioters. In the wake of the riot, a sense of belonging to Hong Kong was also being engineered from above, through the colonial government's social reforms in housing, education, community services, political consultation, and anti-corruption. Above all, the 1967 riot etched an entrenched moral boundary between lawfulness (us, Hong Kongers) and violence (them, Mainland Chinese) in the city's collective consciousness. Aversion to violence and adherence to the law became a political dogma marking all subsequent protests, only to come undone at the seam by the younger generations of activists in the 2010s.

The million-strong protests on May 21 and May 28, 1989, marked another iconic moment in the making of Hong Kong as a political community achieved through the othering of China. Emerging from a period of political uncertainty in the early 1980s when Hong Kong's future was determined by rounds of Sino-British negotiations without Hong Kong's participation, and as Hong Kong citizens nervously braced for their imposed "return to the motherland," Chinese students' pro-democracy agitation struck an emotional chord. The military crackdown felt too much like an ominous rehearsal foretelling Hong Kong's future. Tiananmen was experienced as an epic struggle between good and evil, and citizens built a sense of unity on the ground of their moral clarity. The June 4th vigil held in Hong Kong's Victoria Park that year would last for the next three decades as an essential fixture in Hong Kong's annual political calendar, attended by anywhere between 40,000 to 180,000 people each year. It stood for a society's refusal to forget or whitewash the regime's killing of its own people and its insistence on resurrecting the righteousness of the Tiananmen protest, countering the amnesia enforced by the Mainland regime. Positioning itself as "an untamable internal critic of China," Hong Kong's historical subjectivity grew out of "a kind of Chinese identity, but because Hong Kong is the only place that allows people to own the mission of 'justice for June 4 victims,' their June 4 memories became an indispensable element of the local political consciousness and carried a special meaning to the 'Hongkonger' identity" (Law 2017: 25).

If many were "baptized through June 4th," they were empowered by "July 1st 2003," a third protest event that transformed collective subjectivity and regime governance. As explained earlier, the immediate cause was people's demand for the withdrawal of Article 23 legislation intended to drastically curtail civil liberty in the name of national security. Exceeding everyone's expectations, including those of the citizens themselves, half a million people poured into the streets to express their grievances against the chief executive whose administration was also blamed for Hong Kong's economic distress, collapse in the property market, and SARS-induced social suffering. Braving the scorching sun and the sea of humanity that clogged downtown streets for hours on end, organizers and marchers all took pride in Hong Kong's protest style – massive but orderly, patient but determined, outraged but law-abiding – and substance – demands for liberty, justice, human rights, and democracy. There was no damage of property, no scuffle with the police or other protestors, only resounding and cheerful chants of slogans such as "Power to the people," "Universal suffrage for election of CE," "No to Article 23," and "Down with Old Tung." It should be emphasized that the blame for Hong Kong's distress was squarely laid on the SAR administration, and Beijing, whose main misstep was appointing

Tung, was looked upon ambivalently by the protesters. Still keeping its promise of allowing a high level of autonomy for Hong Kong, Premier Wen Jiabao was not made a target even though he happened to be visiting Hong Kong the morning of the protest.

People were mostly self-mobilized by their social networks and social media, not NGOs or political parties. The organizer, the Civil Human Rights Front, was remarkable for its failure to anticipate the overwhelming turnout. The protest's empowerment effect was augmented by the Government's concession to with-draw the bill, and the subsequent resignation of two top officials responsible for this policy debacle. The protest "changed the Chinese government's perceptions of the political situation in the city, the local public's perceptions of the possibility of effecting political change through their collective action, and the political elite's perceptions of the need to respond to 'public opinion.' Suddenly, people began to imagine the previously unimagined or unimagin-able" (Lee and Chan 2011: 9). As a focus group participant explained, "I'm just a little citizen, but I can make a placard out of a cardboard and speak my mind. I can call [the Chief Executive] a real jerk, I can demand anything. All voices can be represented" (Lee and Chan 2008: 95). Each year since 2003, the annual official commemoration of July 1 as Hong Kong's return to China has been appropriated by civil society to remember what local media discourses has coined the "July 1 effects" and "July 1 spirits." Depending on the political climate each year, anywhere between 20,000 and upward of 550,000 citizens showed up for the march.

Like any ceremony, the annual June 4th vigil and July 1st rally cost citizens little in terms of time, resources, or commitment. Habituation to the ritualistic protest also implies the lack of radicalization on the part of protesters and activists. For all their empowerment effect and cognitive affirmation of the city's core values, people's conservative reformist aspiration was underscored by their adamant insistence on orderly and lawful behavior. The city's major English newspaper articulated a mainstream view in one of its editorials: "

> The SAR is founded on the rule of law and thrives because of it. People cannot pick and choose which sections of the law they want to obey. When laws are repressive, they can be challenged, but a free society has legal means of bringing about change. That is the better cause. In a democracy, public pressure should influence government without resorting to law-breaking.
>
> (*South China Morning Post*, October 26, 2000)

Energized by the success of the July 1, 2003 protest, the democrats won big in the legislative council and district board elections in its immediate aftermath. An institutionalized path to electoral democratization seemed possible and preferable, so much so that even previous antiestablishment figures with anarchic persuasions such as the iconic activist Long Hair, chose to participate in elections. "We saw an electoral path, an institutional blueprint toward full democratization. So we thought we should just follow it, to fight step by step . . .," recalled long-time democrat Lee Chuek Yan in 2021, explaining their faith in electoral reform in favor of protests two decades ago. For ordinary citizens, the Hong Kong economy began to recover, taking advantage of China's sustained economic growth after its accession to WTO and the influx of Chinese tourists. The world economy embraced China which provided a much-needed new growth pole to absorb chronic problems of overcapacity and falling profits. Western powers subscribed to the belief that economic integration would peacefully transform China politically and culturally into their own image. Hong Kong, serving as the bridge of China and the West, rode on this global wave of neoliberal capitalist expansion and was an integral part of this mutual embrace.

The initial ruptures, epitomized by the June 4 vigil and the July 1 rally, were moments of cognitive liberation and collective effervescence from which emerged an imagined community of Hong Kongers bonded by shared values. But beyond these two annual rituals, Hong Kong citizens accepted Chinese rule as a political reality enshrined in the Sino-British Declaration, an international treaty. Their Chinese cultural descent, encouraged by the colonial government as an alternative to nationalism, also fostered an affective identity with China. The most revealing moment of Hong Kongers' affective attachment to their Chinese identity came in 2008 when the Sichuan earthquake and the Beijing Olympics brought forth massive donations and expressions of pride, respectively. Ambivalence toward Chinese sovereignty and identity would morph into sharper divides in the ensuing decade through a number of eventful protests going much beyond annual rituals. Beginning as fringe mobilizations by environmentalists and young idealistic social and cultural workers, a culture of protests would take hold, and a new repertoire of contention, a new generation of activists, and a new political imagination would emerge. I call this period (2003–19) "localism unbound" to highlight the spectrum of "localist" ideologies and strategies to assert Hong Kongers' rights, interests, and autonomy. Different shades of localism developed in response to three forces: internal colonization by Mainland China, neoliberal capitalist capture of space and livelihood, and the exhaustion of the paradigm of institutionalized politics emphasizing negotiation with China. As a politics of belonging, localism is about rights and power as much as moral commitment, affection, and attachment to a place-based community.

3.4 Localism Unbound: Politics of Belonging (2003–19)

This period of "localism unbound" is to be distinguished from its antecedent in the 1990s, when popular culture and intellectual debates raised the question of local Hong Kong identity, against the background of Hong Kong's impending handover to Chinese sovereignty. Scholars and commentators adopted the lenses of postcolonialism and cosmopolitanism to affirm the hybrid nature and subversive mentality of Hong Kong pop culture, and explore Hong Kong's relations with China and the world through a self–other relationship (Law 2017: 26–27). Cultural localism, in films, music, literature, or cultural criticism, soon gave way to localist political movements from 2003 to 2019 in response to global China and neoliberalism. What follows is both an account of how a variety of localist claims and their action strategies grew through and from protest events as well as the range of political agents pushing for change.

3.4.1 Claims: Varieties of Localism

Paradoxically, the SAR government's policy to promote Hong Kong as a global city played a central role in fostering localist demands. Reeling from the 1997 Asian financial crisis and facing the collapse of the real estate market in its aftermath, the government partook in the global trend of developing a "cultural economy," that is, turning culture, arts, and heritage into tourism and retail industries. In a bid to make Hong Kong "Asia's world city," historical buildings were identified and refurnished for cultural, community, entertainment, and commercial uses, with the private sector bearing the cost and capturing the profits of redevelopment. Inadvertently, the government's policy and discursive emphasis on heritage and local culture spurred community interests in their own collective memories and local history. Several prominent campaigns were launched between 2003 and 2010 targeting the demolition or commercialization of heritage architecture and historic neighborhoods. These included the campaign against reclamation in Victoria Harbor (creating space for prime real estate but significantly narrowing the harbor), demolition of the Central Police Compound (the first colonial structure built in 1841 symbolizing the early colonial criminal justice system), the Wedding Card Street (a neighborhood housing a cottage industry specialized in the printing of wedding cards), the Star Ferry Pier (an iconic and busy pier with a Westminster-style clock tower), the Queen's Pier (a colonial ceremonial structure for the landing of colonial governors and British royalties), and Tsoi Yuen Village (a small community of elderly farmers slated for clearance to make way for a high-speed rail connecting

Kowloon to the Mainland). Leveraging the power of the newly available social media space, a small number of journalists, writers, intellectuals, social workers, academics, and students launched these campaigns and succeeded in creating disproportionately broad societal and discursive impacts.

These self-styled "progressive localists" claimed that these buildings and spaces embodied the story of Hong Kong and of being Hong Kongers. They posited an opposition between, on the one hand, "people's" space in the dual sense of common folks and autonomous citizens demanding participatory planning, and, on the other, urban developmentalism imposed by a business–government growth coalition. The term "collective memory" gained currency in the mass media, which churned out sentimental accounts of citizens' personal experiences (e.g. first dates along the waterfront) of public spaces slated for demolition. Activists such as Eddie Chu (mentioned in Section 1), Chan King Fai, and Ip Iam Chong reminded people that the 1966 hunger strike took place at the Star Ferry Pier, and that the Wedding Cards Street and the Tsoi Yuen village, respectively, represented a local folk industry and an alternative lifestyle eliminated by undemocratic planning. According to two activist academics (Chen and Szeto 2015) heavily involved in these mobilizations, their agenda was "preserving now" by promoting people's reidentification with the locality and regaining control over everyday life in situ, to be liberated from neoliberal commercialization and statist colonial past. Their brand of localism was anchored in territorial, communal, and cultural practices, informed by a notion of everyday politics outside the confines of constitutional democracy or rights-based social movements.

Following the government's determination to press ahead with the various redevelopment projects, this brand of anti-capitalist localism subsided, but a new wave of anti-China localism emerged. These two strands of localism shared the same grievances about the unequal right to access and use public and spatial resources but they construed the "local" through different "others" – corporate and political elite in the former, and Mainland Chinese pregnant women, tourists, parallel traders, and immigrants in the latter.

Anti-China localism, targeting Mainland Chinese as unwelcome invaders, or "yellow locusts," competing with Hong Kong citizens for scarce resources, was championed by young people confronting stagnant wages and high property prices. It was, in essence, a class war aggravated by and experienced as a Hong Kong–China confrontation. As Hui and Lau (2015: 354) perceptively argued:

> (A)s a consequence of the disparity in the distribution of time, space, and cultural capital, it is the majority low-income and resource-scarce groups that

are at the forefront to absorb the impacts caused by the large-scale invasion of capital and political power, as well as millions of visitors from mainland China, along with all the most immediate disturbances of everyday life. They are more susceptible to the exclusive (anti-Chinese) sentiments, compared with the sectors with higher income and have more access to various types of opportunities and resources.

Localism for the anti-China activists literally means "Hong Kong people first" in material and livelihood terms: hospital beds in maternity wards for local mothers rather than birth tourists, mass transits serving the commuting needs of residents rather than Mainland visitors, neighborhood shops selling daily necessities for locals rather than baby milk powder purchased in bulk by suitcase-bearing parallel traders. Invoking the term "reclaim" to describe their protests in various border towns from 2011 to 19, this brand of localism featured explicit xenophobic and exclusionary tendencies also found in contemporary populist right movements elsewhere. But in Hong Kong, thanks to the official policy of deepening economic and social integration with the Mainland, the crux and sources of problems were attributed to the influx of Mainland Chinese. Writings (e.g. Chin Wan) promoting nativist, chauvinist ideology attracted a following, even though their claims that Hong Kong is a city state based on ethnic cultural identification are often contradictory and incoherent (Veg 2017: 329–330).

Paralleling the development of anti-Mainland localism, and as Beijing made determined strides in remolding young minds in Hong Kong through nationalistic school curriculum and disenfranchising citizens' right to universal suffrage, a third strand of localism made a claim for Hong Kong's political autonomy and self-determination. Fong (2017) terms this peripheral nationalism, an ideology reacting against Mainland China's assimilationist state-building nationalism. This mode of localism defines Hong Kong as a political community sharing civic values that are distinct and under threat from Chinese intervention. In the protests against the proposed moral and national education curriculum (2011–12), the student leader Joshua Wong wrote, "we decided to fight for freedom of speech and not brainwashing ideology of patriotism," (cited in Adorjan and Yau 2015: 165). Parents in this protest movement similarly contrasted a "lying generation" that the national education textbooks would create with their aspiration for an open-minded generation capable of critical thinking. The protesters criticized the proposed curriculum's goal to promote ethnic identification with China as one based on affect, rather than knowledge and rational engagement.

By the time the 2014 Umbrella Movement rolled around, China had become the "other" for all three camps of Hong Kong localists. The most immediate cause of the seventy-nine-day occupation movement was Beijing's decision to abrogate the Basic Law blueprint to move toward universal suffrage for the election of the chief executive and its insistence on "patriotism" as a criterion for political and judicial appointments. Localism gained tremendous traction among the Umbrella Movement participants, 80 percent of whom professed their sole identification as "Hongkongers" (as opposed to "Chinese" or "Hong Kong Chinese"). For them, democracy and localism were one and the same. As the Communist regime increasingly demanded ethno-cultural identification in its self-legitimizing discourse, incorporating traditional culture and Confucian concepts and extolling blood ties, the Umbrella protesters defined their Hong Kong identification in civic terms, rejecting the essentialism implicit in the CCP's ethno-nationalism (Veg 2017: 327). A student contributor to a collection of essays expounding the idea of Hong Kong nationalism maintained that "Hong Kong nationalism must steer clear of narrow racial nationalism, and use identification with values rather than with blood. In keeping with geography, history and other objective conditions, respecting the freedom of individual agreement, [we must] foster a kind of civic nationalism" (cited in Veg 2017: 340).

Animating the seventy-nine days of occupation across three sites in downtown Hong Kong were debates and slogans about "The Hong Kong nation/ people deciding its destiny," "subjectivity," "agency," "autonomy" (自主), "self-determination" (自決), and "masters of our own destiny" (命運自決). Repudiating an older generation of activists' "reunion in democracy" agenda, student protesters spoke for many of their generation when they sharply demarcated their and the older generations' understanding of Hong Kong's democracy struggle in relation to China: "The Umbrella movement was a democratic movement for Hong Kong. The imagined community was Hong Kong. Not democracy in China, or democracy in Hong Kong to promote democracy in China. Martin Lee did not understand this when he said the Umbrella movement was part of the Chinese democracy movement" (Veg 2017: 341). Importantly, the imprints of these political ideas on the collective consciousness of the "umbrella generation" would outlast the movement.

After the Umbrella Movement failed to bring about electoral reform and was literally bulldozed by a court eviction order instigated by pro-Beijing civil society groups, localists sought to channel the palpable popular support for localism from the streets to the legislature. Political parties were formed swiftly one after another in 2015, including Demosisto (formerly Scholarism), the Hong Kong Indigenous, Hong Kong National Party, and Youngspiration. Their charismatic young political leaders, such as Joshua Wong, Nathan Law, Edward Leung, Ray Wong, Baggio Leung, and Yau Wai-ching, among others, infused new energy into and widened the spectrum of the local political landscape. Together with several new politicians without party affiliation and running under the banner of localism, they were collectively called the "third force," echoing their counterparts in Taiwan, and offering an alternative to the extant pro-establishment and pan-democratic political camps. This strand of political localism arose out of people's frustration with and rejection of established pan-democratic parties whose conciliatory and concessionary stance toward China had failed to obtain any tangible progress since the handover (Kwong 2016). Some groups called for protection of local culture and developing national consciousness, others envisioned an array of political options, from a referendum on self-determination to maintaining the SAR status quo after its initial expiry date of 2047, and independence from China. At this stage, "Hong Kong independence" was still a fringe idea considered too radical and unrealistic by the general population. Yet, its most vocal advocate, Edward Leung, was able to win 15 percent of the vote in a LegCo by-election in 2016. His snappy campaign slogan "Liberate Hong Kong, Revolution of Our Times" (meaning fundamental change from below of the existing power structure by all freedom-loving people) would, in 2019, become the signature rallying cry for the six-month-long battle with the regime and take on new political meanings.

3.4.2 Action: Peaceful, Direct, Fun, Artistic, and Militant

Developing in tandem with the various strands of localist thought was an expansive and diversified tool kit of action. The most salient transformation was the gradual emergence and normalization of direct, confrontational, and militant modes of action, offering an alternative to the erstwhile sacrosanct paradigm of peaceful, rational, and nonviolent (和理非)resistance. Also breaking the hegemony of "rational" action was emotional mobilization, or the deliberate appeal to collective feelings such as nostalgia, anger, happiness, playfulness, fun, injustice, and indignation. Finally, culture, art, and performance opened up venues of expressive participation in addition to instrumental ones aimed at generating political pressure through rallies and processions. This expanded and diversified repertoire allowed more citizens to choose their own modes of engagement, producing an aggregate effect of broadening people's sense of ownership of the struggles.

A foundational moment for a paradigm shift in protest repertoire was the 2005 anti-WTO protest in Hong Kong, the site of the WTO ministerial meeting. Once again, the Hong Kong Government's global city agenda was the inadvertent catalyst for innovating local civil society's tactical tool box, just as the same agenda had spurred the rise of localist identities by commercializing cultural heritage. The Secretary for Commerce, Industry and Technology, eager to showcase Hong Kong as a global city, wrote to 147 WTO member countries, lobbying them to support Hong Kong's bid as host. The Government "budgeted about $300 million for the event, hoping it will help raise the city's international profile" (Ho 2004). For about a week in December 2005, more than 2,000 South Korean farmers, together with an alliance of global civil society groups, demonstrated the power of a highly organized, disciplined, versatile, adaptive, and confrontational movement. Proud of their self-mobilized, loosely organized, and law-abiding July 1 marches, Hong Kong activists and citizens alike were mesmerized by this totally different model of protest – occupying roads and public spaces, breaking police cordons, making weapons with onsite objects, building triangular barricades with roadside railings, bracing tear gas canisters with umbrellas and cling wraps, using humble gestures of bowing and kneeling in their marches through town, engaging the public with joyful music and dance performances. It was a revelation and an awakening. In the protests to come, Hong Kongers would lift many pages from the South Korean playbook, mimicking their shrewd combination of militant and peaceful tactics.

In the wake of the anti-WTO protest, between 2006 and 2010, organizers of the Star Ferry Pier, Queen's Pier and Anti-Express Rail protests put into practice what they had witnessed firsthand. They deployed an amalgam of peaceful, rational, confrontational, performative, and contemplative public action. In addition to hosting forums to engage the public in debates with government officials, they also adopted confrontational direct-action strategies: erecting makeshift barricades, occupying public areas, staging hunger strikes, physically confronting the police, charging into the LegCo building, and forming human chains to deter police clearance.

An integral part of these organizers' developing repertoire of contention was emotional mobilization. Collective emotions of outrage, indignation, injustice, hope, and joy were seen as effective carriers of political messages. Protesters strategically hosted exhibitions and seminars at the demolition sites of the Star Ferry and Queen's Pier to reframe local historical narratives, organized cultural tours complete with home-made meals to the little village slated for demolition in the Anti-Express Rail protests, and published sentimental oral histories of humble elderly farmers on social and independent media. The choreographed ascetic march was aimed at attracting people and "touching them emotionally," according to the organizers. Around 400 young people, dressed in black and white, spent four days walking through five districts – twenty-six kilometers every day, which equals the distance of the railway segment in the Hong Kong territory. With drumbeats in the background, they went down on their knees after every twenty-six slowly proceeding steps. Their performance reminded the audiences, as well as the performers, of ideal and imaginations tied to the local land while seeds were sowed onto the asphalt road in the commercial heart of Hong Kong. The group's adoption of artistic performance was aimed at inciting Hongkongers with peace and ideals rather than a notion of fear (Man 2017).

Relatedly, "joyous resistance" or "happy fighting" became a popular protest style in the 2010s. In addition to the "Fun and Greenery Cultural Festival" during the anti-Express Rail protests, the small but radical political party People's Power adopted it to attract thousands of participants. For instance, they led supporters to play "hitting the villain" (slapping a piece of paper with the name of the villain with a plastic slipper) to express dissatisfaction with the government. Playing yo-yo created similar protest effect:

> After the chorus of cries demanding democratic elections had echoed through the streets for nearly two hours, the leaders prepared a Chinese yo-yo, symbolizing a small circle election, for their supporters to play with. When the followers played with the yo-yo together, it signified that they were throwing the small circle election away . . . a sense of amazement was created while playing the game. (Ng and Chan 2017: 99)

In this age of connective action, when digital media are the organizing agents, it is only natural that social mobilizations in Hong Kong have been less and less defined by clear and recognized leaders. Instead, "social media offer a connective logic in which personal action frames take center stage. This, in turn, results in an aesthetic cacophony of voices, sounds, and images" and "an intense visualization and spectacularization" of protests (de Kloet 2018: 163). An explosion of concentrated artistic and creative expressions accompanied many protests. An early example was the theatrical display to decolonize the Queen's Pier and to transform it from a royalty's to a people's landing site:

> [A hundred] people from various under-represented groups . . . on a rented medium-sized fishing boat named "Localism" . . . imitated the disembarking ceremony of the colonisers at the Queen's Pier. The boat-riders arrived at the Queen's Pier and reclaimed the place as not just being "the Queen's Pier," but also being the Hongkongers' Pier. Flags and decorations were set up to resemble the grand colonial ceremonies from the 1970s. (Man 2017: 8)

The seventy-nine days of occupation during the Umbrella Movement provided fertile and stable ground for protest art to flourish. Making art in situ broke the monotony of physical occupation, and galvanized and sustained participants' interests and morale. Since the image of the humble yellow umbrella was widely disseminated early on as the protesters' ubiquitous defensive tool against the police, it became the central motif in different forms of protest art through the occupied sites – songs, installation art, dance performance, drawings, graffiti, origami, slogans, poems. The rich textual and artistic worlds created during the Umbrella Movement drew inspirations and icons from a synthesized repertoire consisting of global, Chinese, and local sources, from world religions to pop cultures East and West (Veg 2017; Ho 2019). It is ironic that protest art as a peaceful, nonphysical and undisruptive way of political participation had the effect of radicalizing protests in the sense of recruiting a larger segment of the general population, both local and international, into the struggles. As one ethnographer recalled,

> The public and the international audience were drawn to the creative use of popular cultural icons, creative photography works, digitally-created original works, performance art forms, and other entertaining ways of expressing their democratic beliefs. This was combined with the organized ways in which the protestors cleaned up the streets on 6 October 2014, apologized to members of the public for their inconvenience, and quietly go about doing their homework at the protest square. All these images emanate soft power to the local and global audience through concepts of social responsibility, democratic ideals, and quiet strength. (Lim 2015: 93)

The same period also witnessed the gradual mainstreaming of militancy. Emerging as a fringe force during the Umbrella Movement, the use of physical confrontation with the police and with opposition movements was initially condemned for introducing violence and sectarianism, and deviating from Hong Kongers' core value of respecting law and order. The struggle between these two broad action orientations drove a pernicious wedge within the Umbrella Movement, and manifested as verbal and physical fights among different factions on protest sites. Yet, beyond the Umbrella Movement, aggressive provocation was the method of choice among activists of more than thirty restoration protests since 2011. Reaching a peak in 2014 and 2015, and rallying around the banners of anti-Mainlandization and anti-colonization, crowds of several hundred people would roam around shopping malls or commercial districts frequented by Mainland tourists in border towns such as Shatin, Tun Mun, Yuen Long, and Sheung Shui. Claiming to be spontaneous and unorganized shoppers, refusing to seek police approval for their gathering, they verbally harassed Mainlander-looking visitors and kicked the suitcases of parallel traders. Emotions and violent scuffles flared up when pro-China groups and triads joined the fight to defend Mainlanders.

Then came the Mongkok riot on February 8, 2016. It was Chinese New Year's eve, and localist groups called on the public to support the local stall economy and street vendors. When sanitation officers raided the night market of Mongkok, known for its many fishball vendors, clashes between the police and the public turned violent over the ensuing hours. According to court documents, among the estimated 500 bystanders, some 70 or so people threw bricks, glass bottles, and wooden poles at the police who were initially outnumbered, but were later reinforced by riot police and tactical squads. About ten participants holding shields and wearing the outfit of the political party Hong Kong Indigenous, including the charismatic leaders Edward Leung and Ray Wong, gave orders to the crowd to charge toward the police who responded with pepper spray and batons. Protesters also burned trash cans and other onsite materials to form barricades and assaulted the police with various objects. The frustration and alienation of the younger generations reached a zenith and morphed into a wider popular acceptance of militancy. "Despite the violent outcome, Leung's leadership in the unrest gained popularity and sympathy, not only from those who were sympathetic to the localist cause but also from some in the traditional pro-democracy camp. Eventually, Leung captured 15% of the vote in a by-election of the Legislature a few months later, an indication that he would stand a high chance of winning the upcoming general election" (Yuen and Chung 2018), had he not been disqualified for his pro-independence stance. All told, during the Mongkok riot, eighty-five people sustained injuries, thirty were convicted of rioting and assault, and handed heavy sentences of up to seven years in prison.

3.5 Regime's Turn to Institutional Violence

As Hong Kong citizens dramatically enriched the city's repertoire of localist ideology and action in the period between 2003 and 2018 in response to Beijing's ever deepening interventions, the SAR government and its pro-China allies resorted to an increasingly violent arsenal of counter tactics. At the beginning, progressive localists protesting at the Star Ferry and Queen's Pier, and students and parents occupying the Civic Square to protest against curriculum reform, were removed from the sites by police, without being charged. During the Umbrella Movement, tear gas and pepper spray were used, alongside staged pro-establishment rallies where participants were paid by shifts. The regime also outsourced both physical assaults on protesters to thugs and application for court orders to clear the occupation site to pro-Beijing business associations (E. Lee 2020). When the momentum of localism as a political force veering toward independence proved to be too blatant an affront to China's claim of sovereignty, the use of institutional violence became routine. One by one, young localist politicians were disqualified by the government either as candidates or as elected legislators, on the respective grounds of their independence-leaning campaign platforms or their unconventional behavior in the swearing-in ceremony. Some of them were imprisoned or forced into exile for their roles in the 2016 Mong Kok riot. Beijing's unabashed political persecution of young localists effectively deprived the post-80s and post-90s generations of institutionalized political representation, paving the road for radicalization outside the legislature.

Descending into an abeyance, social and political mobilizations lost steam in the next few years when Beijing's control over Hong Kong was intensified. In 2018, when the government announced the "colocation" plan to allow extra-territoriality for Mainland Chinese customs and law enforcement within the Express Rail Terminal in downtown Kowloon, public outrage against Chinese colonization was reignited. Yet, mass fatigue and sense of powerlessness stymied the turnout of demonstrations and only about a few hundred citizens showed up to protest. Nobody, therefore, foresaw the groundswell of political activism a few months later when the government proposed an amendment of the extradition bill. Once again, the power of "event" as sudden ruptures unleashing political creativity and agency would change the course of Hong Kong politics.

3.6 "Endgame": What Was Different in 2019?

The Section has argued that the claims for liberty, local autonomy, and democracy, and the mix of peaceful, militant, artistic, and emotional mobilizational tactics propelling the 2019 protests were the culmination of a two-decade-long process. But 2019 was also a transcendence of previous contestations in three ways. First, the regime had hardened its stance toward popular protests by deploying disproportionate force from day one. Never before had police violence played such a major catalyst role in uniting and radicalizing protesters. Second, activists promoted a now-or-never "endgame" mentality, perhaps in light of the anticipated endpoint of "One Country, Two Systems" in 2047, giving this agitation a singular urgency and historical meaning, raising the stakes for both regime and civil society. Desperation and determination compelled many to innovate and to kindle an inclusive solidarity. Third, the international context in 2019 was starkly different from the previous two decades. China's relation with the West had shifted from one of strategic engagement to one of strategic competition. A global backlash against China has become palpable in the forms of a trade war, diplomatic conflicts, and soft power contests. Hong Kong's protests became embroiled in this global rift between China and the West. Global media attention was a boon to the protests and spurred both regime and protesters to dig in.

3.6.1 Police Violence

Until 2019, protest policing in Hong Kong leaned more toward community policing than securitization, emphasizing communication and negotiation, political neutrality, and minimum force. This was the case during the 2006–10 protests against pier demolitions and express rails (Lam 2015). Even during the Umbrella Movement in 2014, police violence was by and large limited to the use of tear gas for crowd dispersal. Police officers who assaulted protesters were prosecuted. The government mainly resorted to "attrition" or mobilized the criminal justice system to inflict institutional violence on activist leaders. Yet, in 2019, the regime reacted with a full-throttled police force ready to inflict disproportionate and indiscriminate physical violence on peaceful demonstrators on June 12, just a few days after the first massive million-strong march. By mid-July, police tactics saw an obvious shift from dispersal to kettling and then to outsourced violence, mass arrests, and brutality toward protesters. The special tactical squad, nicknamed "the raptors," formed originally in response to the Umbrella movement in 2014, was deployed alongside riot police on a daily basis. Their abuse of excessive force triggered an overwhelming sense of violation, injustice, and outrage across class, gender, age, and ethnic divides. Dates like July 14 (attack in a Shatin shopping mall), July 21 (indiscriminate attack by thugs on subway passengers in Yuen Long while the police turned a blind eye), and August 31 (police attack of subway passengers in Mongkok) were etched in public memory because of the extreme scale and severity of violence committed by law enforcement. Police atrocities (e.g. beating protesters with batons and fists even when they were already restrained, sexual harassment, physical abuse under police custody) committed and condoned in a global city renowned for its rule of law stunned the world, and were well documented by Amnesty International and the international media including the *New York Times* and the *Guardian*.

According to policing expert Clifford Stott, the police use of tear gas on June 12 was a tipping point for a shift in protest norms and underlying protester identity. Not only did police violence become the rally cry in almost all protests,

> "Illegitimate and undifferentiated police action created the psychological unity where previously diverse groups with different tactics began to coexist more successfully in order to achieve their common goals. This unity appears to have empowered radical groups perhaps because of the increasing expectation and realization of common support ... Police tactics then served to legitimize and empower escalating acts of community resistance which amplified ever more intensive forms of police repression until the cycle was broken following the siege of the Polytechnic University in December.
>
> (Stott et al. 2020: 19)

Besides fostering unity, police violence expanded the base of the movement. As tear gas cannisters were shot in residential neighborhoods and shopping malls, even self-proclaimed apolitical citizens and regime supporters were alienated.

Residents in high-rises and in neighborhoods in downtown protest areas became sympathetic refuge providers to black-bloc youngsters fleeing from riot police. Or they formed agitated impromptu human cordons, wielding their phone cameras as weapons, demanding the release of young people being stopped and frisked by police on the streets. When blue-dyed water cannon was applied to a major mosque in Kowloon, the enraged south Asian Muslim community pledged solidarity with the protesters. During the first months of the movement, the elderly were regular participants in marches and assemblies, and were seen many times at the frontline shouting out loud their complaints against police brutality, asking "why being young is a crime?"

This broad sense of ownership of the movement was accompanied by an endgame mentality that lent an unprecedented urgency to the 2019 struggle. When police violence plunged the city into a civil-war-like scenario, especially after the violent police raids at two university campuses in November resulting in numerous injuries and arrests, talks of "now or never," "point of no return," and "the last battle" became viral in social media, Lennon Wall memo notes, and protest propaganda. The reasoning was that if this battle was lost, that ground would never be regained, and Beijing would not tolerate rebellion of this scale happen again. The dominant slogan of the protest also escalated from "five demands, not one less" to "Hong Kong independence, the only way out." A self-conscious sense of making history, defining this movement as once-in-a-life-time opportunity, a historic watershed for Hong Kong, steeled many people's resolve, especially the younger generation's. Many in the frontline quit jobs or school so they could devote full time to the movement, saying there would be no personal future if Hong Kong had none.

Discursive inventions flourished and deepened the emotional tenor of the 2019 mobilization. For the first time, "martyrs" 義士 appeared in Hong Kong's political lexicon. The term was first used to honor the five people who committed protest suicides and those arrested in the first weeks of street demonstrations. It soon acquired an expansive meaning to include mysterious deaths of young people known to have participated in protests, protesters penning last letters before going to the frontline, and many anonymous victims of police violence in the Mongkok subway attack. Makeshift shrines for people to pay homage were erected at the locations of their deaths, and a mass cemetery for the anonymous was visited on traditional holidays for the dead. In Hong Kong as elsewhere, martyrdom as a "totemic" act transformed grief and bereavement into a sacrificial ideal through a commemorative community which produced meaning and solidarity out of death. And if the sovereign wielded power of decisions over life and death, then martyrdom presented its ultimate resistance (Fordahl 2018). Finally, a related term of endearment 手足 literally meaning "hands and feet" was universally used to refer to brothers and sisters in action, as well as the more than 10,000 arrested for participating in protests. On the street, the ubiquitous appellations of "hands and feet" signaled equality, camaraderie, intimacy, and mutuality among strangers.

3.6.2 Reflexivity and Solidarity

The unprecedented scale and sustainability of mass support for the 2019 protests stemmed partly from the societal unity in response to state violence, but also from the protesters' capacity for reflexivity and solidarity. Reflexivity about past fragmentation was a popular topic of discussion at the virtual headquarters of the movement (i.e. LIHKG and Telegram channels). A consensus was forged in the early days of the movement that this time people must overcome the acrimonious division between the militants and the pacifists that doomed the Umbrella Movement. One of the most popular posts appealing for solidarity appeared on LIHKG on June 17, 2019. It has since been censored and is no longer available, but is provided here for interest.

> To the happy resisters (meaning the pacifists): Hong Kong will never obtain any government concession if we only resist with fun and playfulness. But your power is very important because you have public opinion support and can move people's emotion, to plant the seed of democracy by teaching their children about democracy. Your job is to cement public support, and focus on good propaganda. To the militants: you are the big winners of this movement because people now recognize your action brought results. You should focus on fighting well each street battle and not on condemning the futility of the happy resisters. Militancy without popular consent will definitely be criticized as riots. Pacifists' propaganda warfare can be a very useful supplementary side attack for you.

Other popular posts that were voted up by many on LIHKG talked about the importance of "not repeating the mistakes of the Umbrella," and urged Hong Kongers to learn from Mao Zedong's theory of uniting all secondary enemies to fight the primary enemy. "Hong Kong failed in past movements because it was a puddle of sand, with lot of internal strife" (June 22, LIHKG). As cycles of heated debate emerged over the course of the movement, keyword count of slogans emphasizing the cardinal principle of solidarity also jumped exponentially. These slogans include: "Five Demands, Not One Less," "climbing the same mountains, each contributes his efforts, going up and down together," "no splitting, no condemnation, no snitching," and "no big stage, no leaders" (F. Lee 2020).

A signal moment of solidarity between the militants and the pacifists was the storming of the Legislative Council Building on July 1. The protesters broke glass windows, dismantled furniture, daubed graffiti, and defaced portraits of the political elite and the PRC emblem, but they left cash payment for the drinks they took from vending machines, and left the library intact. One slogan sprayed on the walls explained their action: "It's you who taught us peaceful means are useless." Unexpectedly, rather than being condemned, their principled violence won the support of the elderly, housewives, and public opinion. During the siege of the airport, another radical move, when the police were rumored to arrest all the protesters occupying the airport, thousands of citizens participated in a Dunkirk-style rescue action with their own vehicles or taxis. Even when militant action escalated to vandalizing pro-China businesses, frontline protesters' clear moral code in the use of principled violence helped them secure majority public support.

How did protesters achieve solidarity beyond discursive emphasis? Durkheim's concepts of collective effervescence, and mechanical and organic solidarity are illuminating of the Hong Kong experience. Months of massive participation in rallies and confrontations offered many citizens an opportunity to feel, in the presence of fellow citizens, the empowerment and camaraderie in collective resistance as well as achieve a kinetic appreciation for the bravery and sacrifice of the young frontliners. Affective, moral, and emotional integration, or mechanical solidarity, were kindled and rekindled over a six-month battle, expressed in the same set of political demands for civic liberty and freedom chanted in all protests.

Then there was organic solidarity. Citizen cohesion arose also from an elaborate division of labor and mutual reliance on each other for specialized task performance during episodes of collective action. Social media platforms such as Telegram channels and LIHKG circulated a manual listing twenty "occupations" for citizens of all physical strength and personal predilection to choose from. The monikers for these occupations included "dog killer" (frontline attacker), "magician" (Molotov thrower), "fire fighter" (tear gas extinguisher), "weatherman" (blocking cameras with umbrella), "painter" (slogans sprayer), and "school bus driver" (driving getaway cars). Open telegram channels offered instructions on how to perform these tasks while numerous "small teams" were formed to coordinate specific action on a particular day. Or people could pitch in solo, depending on their availability, skill set, and level of risk tolerance. The large number of protests ensured ample practice opportunities among citizens whose participation was anonymous, flexible, and attuned to a highly decentralized and fluid action context. In short, it was not just technological affordance but willful historical reflexive agency that brought about a solidarity culture and a community in action.

3.6.3 Tactical Creativity

The 2019 movement broke new ground in the annals of Hong Kong's protest history in terms of tactical creativity. The three new tactics – new unionism, the yellow economic circle, and international diplomacy – challenged key components of Hong Kong's entrenched power structure and together intimated an embryonic vision for a new society, economy, and diplomacy. In this sense, the slogan "revolution of our times" was remarkably prescient.

Five months into the movement, and in the wake of the mysterious deaths of Chow Tsz-lok and Chan Yan-lin, two youngsters known to have participated in protests, the city was shaken and inflamed with anger. Beginning in early November, the protest slogan "Hong Kongers, add oil" took a dark turn to "Hong Kongers, take revenge." Protesters resorted to more disruptive action in order to force a general strike into existence. The police retaliated with ferocious attacks on two university campuses whose locations allowed protesters to choke traffic in the city. Hong Kong descended into an urban war zone, with mounting injuries and arrests. These physical confrontations were so intense that many peaceful and nonmilitant protesters were desperate to find alternative means to continue the movement without "sending more people to the guillotines." New unionism was their answer to this emergency situation. The idea of forming unions to realize a general strike was promoted by independent unionists right from the beginning of the movement in June. To respond to the call for general strikes in August and September, many protesters initiated and joined Telegram groups formed along industrial and occupational lines which would later become the preparation committees for new unions. But the avalanche of new union formation only took off after the siege at the two universities, and by early 2020, officials confirmed that some 1,600 new unions had submitted paperwork for registration and the obstructionist government warned that it would take fifty years to process them! This new wave of unionism was remarkable for its youthful and educated leadership, the prevalence of professional occupations represented, and its political motivation and agenda. The formation brought new energy to the marginalized independent union movement and challenged the complacency of the co-opted pro-Beijing unions. Most important of all, organizers wanted to leverage the institutional legitimacy and organizational potential of unionism to counter red capital and to bring democracy to the workplace and everyday life.

Another tactical innovation to broaden the terrain of struggle was the practice of supporting pro-movement businesses and to develop an economic supply chain independent of Mainland China and its red capital. This political consumption movement, called the "yellow economic circle," like other forms of solidarity economy the world over, leveraged ordinary citizens' purchasing power to build the economic foundation for a political cause. By challenging the entrenched ideology of market Darwinism, and the domination of oligopolistic local and red capital, the yellow economic circle opened the market niche for local entrepreneurs and their small businesses. Directories of yellow businesses counted some 6,000 entities in 2020, about half of which were restaurants. Informational flyers were posted in public places, differentiating for the public "made in China" brands from "ABC" (anything but China) alternatives across numerous categories of consumer products.

Finally, 2019 saw the opening of an international frontline for Hong Kong protests. Whereas the anti-national education campaign and the Umbrella Movement already received overseas support thanks to global digital connectivity, the 2019 movement was the first to make international lobbying a deliberate protest strategy. It began in June 2019 with the stunning success of a crowdfunding initiative to raise HK$ 5 million in a matter of hours. The fund was used to issue frontpage advertisements in ten major international newspapers appealing to leaders attending the G20 in Osaka to act on the crisis in Hong Kong. Soon, teams of university students and professionals were formed to write and meet legislators in Australia, the United States, the United Kingdom, and the European Union. They also drafted policy proposals urging sanctions against Chinese and Hong Kong officials who violated human rights, and coordinated simultaneous action days with the global network of several dozen diasporic organizations formed prior to or during the 2019 movement. For instance, on September 30, 2019, a rally in Hong Kong against totalitarianism was echoed by solidarity protests held in forty cities in the US, UK, Australia, Canada, Germany, France, Italy, New Zealand, the Netherlands, Norway, South Korea, Taiwan, and other places. Signaling the movement's cosmopolitanism was the sea of national flags as a visual fixture whenever rallies happened. The result was unprecedented international attention on Hong Kong lasting for six months, until the pandemic hit in early 2020. With this international campaign, the Hong Kong public developed its own track of city diplomacy, bypassing the SAR and national governments. Lobbying for sanctions against China and Hong Kong, the international front also popularized the idea of "lamm chau" or mutual destruction. The logic was "if we (Hong Kong) burn (because of China's suppression), you (China) burn with us (because of foreign sanction and the demise of a global financial center under its sovereignty)," which resonated with the "endgame" sentiment in the frontline.

3.6.4 Riding the Global Backlash against Global China

The international wing of the movement scored a landmark success in late November 2019, when the United States passed the Hong Kong Human Rights and Democracy Act stipulating sanctions and monitoring mechanisms on human rights violations in Hong Kong. Seven months later, China responded by imposing the National Security Law on Hong Kong, crushing the movement by mass arrests, criminalization of political opposition, removal of civil liberty, media censorship, and more. In return, Britain, Canada, and Australia announced new policies to facilitate the emigration of Hong Kong citizens' and young professionals and the United States imposed further sanctions on Hong Kong and Chinese officials.

Why had these countries stood by Hong Kong in 2019, whereas they had refrained from taking an explicit stance, let alone rolling out legislations and policies, during the Umbrella Movement just five years earlier? If images of sustained police violence against black-clad young protesters had swayed global public sympathy in favor of Hong Kongers, it was economic rivalry between the West and China that explained foreign governments' willingness to confront China. The codependent relationship between the West, especially the United States, and China since the 1990s that initially facilitated China's rise and US growth, had, over two decades, evolved into a high-stake geopolitical and economic conflict by 2019. Wall Street and corporate America, whose interests in the 1990s drove appeasement with China, now found Beijing's expansion abroad and industrial espionage at home a serious threat (Hung 2020). The financial stimulus Beijing offered to its state-owned companies after the 2008 financial crisis allowed them to expand production and marginalize foreign companies in the global market. As global China's patron-clientelist and soft power footprints expanded to all continents, the West and some of the developing countries increasingly realized the insidious risks China posed to their national security, political system, and core values. Trump's ascendance, hard-line rhetoric, and trade war against China finally unleashed a proverbial "new Cold War."

The contingency of this souring of China's relation with the West was a double-edged sword. It was a providential stroke of good luck to the international diplomacy wing of the anti-extradition movement, but it also hardened CCP's perceived need and justification for enhanced securitization and repression (Greitens 2019) in handling domestic dissent, from Xinjiang to Hong Kong. As explained in the previous section, since the early 2000s, global mass uprisings against autocracy had prompted and justified Beijing's promulgation of a series of national security legislations (Greitens, Lee, and Yazici 2020). The eventual imposition of a draconian National Security Law in Hong Kong happened under this national policy shift that took place at the top leadership years before 2019.

3.7 Conclusion

This section offers a brief history of resistance, spotlighting especially the coming of age of locally born but globally aware political generations who leveraged the power of "events" to open cracks in the structure of domination imposed and sustained by China in the post-1997 era. Through a sequence of eventful protests, activists of successive mobilizations in this David-vs.-Goliath contest fostered new political agencies and imaginations, expanded the repertoire of tactics, learned from past mistakes, and experimented with new ways of organizing, all in interaction with changing regime strategies to contain them. It is also a history of radicalization, in the sense of expanding support across social classes, generations, and ethnic groups, deepening popular consciousness about the structural sources of their grievances, and escalating movement demands from issues to institutions to political structures. Coinciding with a backlash from the West against China's global expansion, the 2019 Hong Kong resistance movement became the frontier of international conflicts. Over time, the center cannot hold, except by force. Hence, the passage of the National Security Law in mid-2020, a nuclear option that was poised to annihilate the movement and ruin Hong Kong's global city status, portending irreparable collateral damage to China.

4 Backlash: Lessons from Hong Kong and Beyond

This Element examines Hong Kong as a paradigmatic case of global China and its discontent, understood as a Polanyian "double movement." We have seen how China's economic statecraft, patron-clientelism and symbolic domination fueled countermovements in Hong Kong. Among the many targets of global Chinese expansion, Hong Kong's situation is particularly paradoxical and therefore restive. Thanks to China's sovereignty and the city's global economic centrality, China has more interest and capacity to dominate Hong Kong than elsewhere. But as citizens of a 155-year-old global city with distinct beliefs, senses of belonging, and institutions, Hong Kongers also have stronger interest and capacity to resist Chinese encroachments.

Analytically, Chinese domination in Hong Kong (along with Xinjiang, Tibet, and Macao) amounts to "colonialism" or "internal colonialism," to be distinguished from mere dependence and asymmetry of power. The key difference between dependency and colonialism is that the latter entails essentially the power of the colonists to transplant and install their political, economic, and sociocultural *institutions* in the colonized territory (Mahoney 2012: 23). "Internal" colonization happens when this power dynamic plays out within the same sovereign jurisdiction over a minority population, defined by culture, or language, race and ethnicity, religion, geography, or level of economic development. This concept has been applied to minority–majority politics in South Africa, Thailand, Sudan, Wales, Brittany, Quebec, Austria-Hungary, Scotland, and Bangladesh; to Native Americans, Blacks, and Chicanos in America, Palestinians in Israel, indigenous peoples in Latin America; and to Stalin's nationalities policy in the Soviet Union (Hechter 1975; Gutiérrez 2004).

Compared to Hong Kong, Tibet and Xinjiang are economically and socially less integrated with developed capitalist economies of the world, and have a long history of sustained religious and ethnic strife against the secular and Han-dominant Communist regime. The conflict between Hong Kong and CCP is not based on ethnicity and religion, but civic and political values such as civil liberty, rule of law, and democracy. Yet, all three Chinese internal colonies experienced similar repressive interventions from Beijing during the first decade of the twenty-first century, and people in all three societies refused to submit to Beijing's political control. Popular resistance had fueled more determined crackdown. If my analysis is correct, it is the accumulation and legitimation imperatives of global China that have augmented Beijing's interventionist and repressive turn in all three internal colonies. We can discern similar methods of power – massive infrastructure project to absorb the Mainland's excess capacity and create economic dependence, political domination by elite incorporation and patron clientelism, migration and settlement of Mainland Chinese, symbolic domination through patriotic education, textbook revisions, media control, framing dissent as terrorism, and more. Until 2020, if for nothing else, China's need for Hong Kong as a global financial center had restrained it from imposing extreme measures such as concentration camps and comprehensive surveillance as those in Xinjiang and Tibet (Byler 2021). And out of these spaces of relative freedom and international connections, Hong Kongers managed to pull off mass defiance more visible and more sustained than that found in Xinjiang in 2009 and Tibet in 2008.

4.1 A Spectrum of Counter-Movements

As global China's restive frontier, Hong Kong resistance movement belogns to a broader spectrum of countermovements. In other parts of the world, reports of communal and labor resistance to global China abound. These include indigenous community protests to mining investments in Latin America (Quiliconi and Vasco 2021), farmers and herders rejecting Chinese land grabs in Sri Lanka and Central Asia (Jardine et al. 2020), unions resisting Chinese acquisition of ports in Greece (Reguly 2019), and labor strife along the Belt and Road in Southeast Asia (Chen 2020). In this section, I highlight studies that reveal some of the less visible dynamics of countering China's economic statecraft, patron-clientelism, and symbolic domination. The agency, capacity, and interest behind these reactions vary, and are shaped by the configurations and balance of political-economic forces at the sectoral, national, or global levels.

4.1.1 Appropriating Economic Statecraft

China's strategy of economic statecraft, or using state investment and loans to bolster political, economic, and diplomatic leverage in other countries, has increased China's influence but also produced mixed results (Yang and Liang 2019). Political opposition in foreign countries and political suspicion related to the state-backed nature of Chinese investment often hinder China's agenda. Also, China's economic statecraft can be appropriated by foreign elites. Debunking what the Western media has anxiously touted as the "Angola model" (i.e. China extends "oil-backed loans" to Angola, exchanging resource for infrastructure), Lucy Corkin (2013) brought to light the hidden negotiating capacity of the Angolan elite in dealing with China. From pricing its oil shipment to China according to international spot price rather than a lower fixed price proposed by China, to thwarting Chinese national oil companies' access to oil equity in Angolan oil fields, negotiating for a higher than usual local contents requirement in Chinese concessional loans, and consciously diversifying its international credit lines from Europe, Brazil, and Canada, the Angolan political elite are far from hapless or helpless. Autocratic and corrupt, but seasoned by decades of involvement in a proxy Cold War and buoyed by peak oil, the Angolan political elite's agency has to be resurrected in any discussion about China in Angola.

Another example of elite appropriation happened in Sudan's oil sector. Chinese oil companies there have to negotiate with shrewd and unyielding politicians from both Sudan and South Sudan. From the beginning, Khartoum was in the driver's seat forcing out American oil interest and imposing a joint venture between China National Petroleum Corporation and other foreign investors from Malaysia, Canada, and later India, in developing Sudanese oilfields. Chinese state-owned oil companies had to negotiate a steep learning curve to operate internationally, to survive civil war-related kidnapping and killings of Chinese personnel and armed attacks by local communities which did not benefit from oil revenues, and negotiating with the new South Sudanese regime to keep pipelines flowing from oil fields in the south to the Red Sea in the north. Jiba's decision to shut down oil production in South Sudan in 2012 was evidence of how vulnerable Chinese state investment can turn out to be in Africa. Through all these, as CNPC expanded beyond Sudan, it also gradually learned to reform its security practices, and expanded its political relations beyond engaging the host government to include opposition parties, religious leaders, national media, and local communities (Patey 2014).

Chinese investment in Zambia's copper mining sector was a classic instance of economic statecraft. Yet, as Chinese state capital was driven by the logic of encompassing accumulation – pursuit of profit, political influence, and mineral access – it had to accommodate to Zambian elite's priorities, whereas other multinational corporations seeking the singular imperative of shareholder value maximization were more mobile. Lee (2017) found that to accrue political capital, the Chinese state-owned mining company in Zambia had demonstrated a commitment to stable copper production in ordinary times and during the 2008 crisis to refrain from retrenchment and production suspension, the immediate responses of other global private investors. Most consequentially, Chinese state investors, at the urging of the Zambian Government, conceded to set up a special economic zone, which satisfied the Zambian elite's long-standing desire to develop the country's capacity for copper value addition. In appropriating Chinese investment for its national development, the Zambian politicians were assisted by the electorate's sentiment of resource nationalism against foreign investors in copper, particularly the Chinese which represented the interest of a foreign nation.

Yet, within the same country, the capacity for countermovement varied across industries. The copper mines' political centrality and their unionized workforce were a stark contrast to Zambia's nonstrategic and informalized infrastructure construction sector (Lee 2017). On the part of the elite, Zambian politicians, without the political pressure of resource nationalism, simply appropriated infrastructure projects for their short-term election campaigns and personal political careers, despite the peril of national insolvency in the future. On the part of labor, informalization in construction deprived workers of the collective capacity commanded by miners in resisting Chinese investors. As a result, Chinese state capital, in the forms of concessional loan projects and state-owned contractors, was able to dominate the industry and create long-term debtor dependence.

4.1.2 Usurping Patron-Clientelism

The Chinese diaspora has been the target of patron-clientelism deployed by the Chinese Communist Party's united front machinery. Yet, emigrant Chinese could also usurp this power dynamic and exploit their brokerage role for private interests, derailing state agendas. Chinese emigrant business leaders, *qiaoling* (侨领), in Laos, for instance, amassed symbolic and political capital by public performance of patriotism and then used their influence to victimize Chinese SOEs and wealthy private investors parachuting into the country without local knowledge. Particularly illuminating is the story about the ASEM Villa project, a high-profile Chinese state-aid project undertaken by a central state-owned construction company to build a cluster of fifty luxurious villas by the Mekong river near downtown Vientiane, providing accommodation for visiting state leaders and their entourage during the ninth Asia–Europe Meeting (ASEM) in 2012. The project fell apart, quite literally due to poor quality of construction, two years after its completion, all because a *qiaoling* was shrewd enough to use his local connections and dual citizenship status to extract huge profits from the project while evading legal responsibility and Chinese state disciplines. The Overseas Chinese Affair Office in Laos was caught in a bind: if the beloved Chinese son in Laos openly fell out of grace, the credibility of the Chinese government would be undermined as well (Chen 2022). While buying loyalty echoes the way in which the Chinese state controls and manages political opinions of its domestic population, overseas the state lacks the power to set the price when bargaining with elite transnational subjects for their collaboration. Consequently, it pays enormous hidden costs which cumulatively may threaten to undermine China's global agenda.

Similar to the Chinese diaspora, local officials in countries hosting Chinese state investors played crucial intermediary roles and their collaboration was not guaranteed. Lu's study (2022) of Chinese state investment in rubber plantations in Laos found that central government agreements were often abrogated at the local level. One such case is the Yunnan state farm, whose failure to navigate and satisfy subnational official interests prevented it from acquiring farm land across different local jurisdictions, despite high-level diplomatic facilitation by the Chinese government. The firm had to establish relations with each provincial government anew, creating costs and delays they hadn't planned for, and even once they obtained provincial approval they still had to then develop a relationship with the district and sometimes even negotiate with villagers for land. Only after years of aligning its interests with those of provincial governments and smallholder farmers did the state farm gain a stronghold in rubber production.

4.1.3 Countering Symbolic Domination

The most controversial and contentious effort by China to gain symbolic power is arguably the global networks of Confucius Institutes (CIs). The expansion of these state-sponsored cultural and language programs attracted vocal criticism from politicians and academics. In the United States, the prominent Chicago anthropologist Marshall Sahlins criticized them as "academic malware" promoting the political influence of the Chinese government under the guidance of the propaganda apparatus of the party-state and threatening the principles of academic freedom and integrity of US higher education. In August 2020, the US Secretary of State Mike Pompeo called the Confucius Institute "an entity advancing Beijing's global propaganda and malign influence campaign on American classrooms and campuses," and designated the CI "a foreign propaganda mission." As China's relations with the West sour, at least forty-five CIs among a total of seventy-five in the United States, all CIs in Sweden, and some in Germany have been closed.

Beyond political backlash unleashed by the elite, ethnographic studies of CIs suggest that China is not achieving symbolic domination or soft power. One study (Repnikova 2022) shows that ordinary Ethiopians engaged the CIs due to pragmatic enticements that had little to do with Chinese culture or values. School administrators embraced the CI project because it created job opportunities for their graduates and offers a symbolic alignment of their institutions with global education community and modernity. For Ethiopian students, Chinese language was a channel for experiencing China as a destination and as an employer. For Chinese teachers, foreign posting was a professional and personal growth opportunity. Such pragmatic enticement may work well in the short run, but it has to face a sustainability crisis due to its strong dependence on China's presence in Ethiopia, the job market for Chinese-language graduates, and rising expectations from host institutions. Anthropologist Jennifer Hubbert's (2019) study of CI-sponsored tours to China also found that Chinese officials' self-conscious engineering of the spectacle of China – glorious ancient Chinese culture and sleek modernity – did not resonate with American students. For them, museum exhibits and celebratory performances of Chinese culture lacked the authenticity they desired and found in night markets selling "bizarre indigestibles." Again, the physical construction of CIs, much as the influx of Chinese investment and the co-optation of the Chinese diaspora, tells only one side of the global China story. Only by reinstating the other side – the variety of countermovements – can its relational dynamic and consequences be revealed.

4.2 Coda: What Next for Hong Kong and Global China?

Twenty-three years after Hong Kong's return to Chinese sovereignty, Beijing dismantled the "One Country, Two Systems" framework by imposing the National Security Law in July 2020. At the law's knife point, major institutions in Hong Kong – legislature, election, civil service, education, mass media, criminal justice system – have been swiftly and blatantly Mainlandized (i.e. following the norms and practices in China). Time-honed rules, integrity, and autonomy of the professions (e.g. accounting, medicine, journalism, teaching) have been compromised by the Mainland requirement of submission to the party-state or its euphemism, "patriotism." All notable opposition political leaders were imprisoned or exiled, with a new crop of Mainland-born Hong Kong citizens and their locally co-opted counterparts to rule Hong Kong with Beijing's blessing. Within a few months in 2021, two major liberal media (*Apple Daily* and *Stand News*) and more than fifty civil society organizations, including some of the most venerable and influential ones, were forced to close. The death of "One Country, Two Systems" removes the institutional foundation of Hong Kong as a global financial hub. As Beijing envisions a self-sustaining domestic economy Hong Kong is being absorbed as one among many Chinese cities in the Greater Bay Area (Pearl River Delta regional economy).

Hong Kong's decolonization struggle has been forced into a dark and potentially long hiatus. An exodus of professionals, liberal intellectuals, public opinion leaders, and middle-class families is underway, mainly to the United Kingdom, Canada, Taiwan, the United States, Australia, and beyond. There is a call to regroup and sustain the liberation movement by working abroad as a global diasporic community. Within Hong Kong, democratic and localist aspirations are compelled to turn to anti-politics – fandom for local popular music, running independent book stores, patronizing yellow businesses, protecting local environment, supporting local films and performers, and solidifying communities of care for political prisoners and their families. Using culture, consumption, and community life as terrains of autonomous development is reminiscent of what happened in South Korea and Taiwan during their respective repressive eras. Hong Kong intellectuals have also promoted Vaclav Havel's inspirational mottos of "living in truth" and "the power of the powerless," urging citizens who remain in Hong Kong to sustain the spirit and practice of resistance in their everyday life with their conscience and moral compass.

The historical experiences of East Asia and Eastern Europe are useful reminders that democratic struggles in abeyance may reemerge as unexpected ruptures, when external and internal conditions change. Yet, whereas the people's movements in Taiwan, South Korea, and Eastern Europe were able to ride the wave of political economic liberalizations in the mid- to late 1980s to topple autocracies, Hong Kong's struggle for decolonization has to confront a global headwind of autocratization and right-wing nationalism. Today, flexing its sovereign big-power muscles, Beijing has time and again rejected the universal values of human rights and democracy. China's insistence on demolishing Hong Kong as a global city even at the pain of sanctions and condemnations by Western powers sends a strong global message that nationalism, recovering "lost" territories, and remolding the international order are China's priorities. Marking the 100th anniversary of the Chinese Communist Party, Xi Jinping warned in his valedictory speech to the nation that "we will never allow any foreign force to bully, oppress, or subjugate us. Anyone who dares try to do that will have their heads bashed bloody against the Great Wall of Steel forged by over 1.4 billion Chinese people."

Such stern and feisty rhetoric had observers predicting rising geopolitical tensions, cybersecurity and data wars, even military conflicts across the Taiwan Strait amidst a grand decoupling of China and the US-led West. However, even when relations between Washington and Beijing are at a low ebb, American and European investment firms are embedding themselves ever more deeply into the Chinese wealth asset markets, forging wealth management partnerships with Chinese state-owned banks.[5] Wall Street continued to tot up a record $1.5 billion in fees from helping Chinese firms with initial public offerings offshore in 2020, and US mutual funds investment in China has increased 43 percent between 2020 and 2021.[6] Some financiers observed that the US–China tension has inadvertently boosted Hong Kong's financial sector because a lot of Mainland companies are now hesitating to list in the United States. This translates into a continuous pipeline of large IPOs in Hong Kong and ultimately into capital inflows.[7]

If history offers any reference, one wonders if beneath the rhetoric of US–China decoupling Hong Kong will continue to survive, even thrive, as it did in the past as a global borderland on the edge of empires. During the 1950s–70s, in

---

[5] www.ft.com/content/d5e09db3-549e-4a0b-8dbf-e499d0606df4

[6] www.bloomberg.com/news/articles/2021-07-12/wall-street-s-6-billion-fee-bonanza-chilled-by-china-ipo-curbs ; www.nytimes.com/2021/10/06/business/china-business-wall-street.html

[7] www.ft.com/content/3dd7c745-e96c-4d43-a90f-b2908f7a2a94

the midst of the Cold War, Hong Kong's betwixt and between position nurtured a cosmopolitan capitalist and educational elite. These entrepreneurial family firms in banking, manufacturing, retailing, wholesaling, and higher education spun flexible networks of commerce integrating Hong Kong into the US and global economy (Hamilton 1999, Hamilton 2021). From such economic and educational infrastructure Hong Kong grew into an urbane and global city with a hybrid culture, as it served the mutual geopolitical and intelligence interests of supposedly archenemies in great power politics. The question now is whether and how Hong Kong and its people, including those in the diaspora, build on its storied cosmopolitanism to find a way out of the fog of this so-called new Cold War.

References

Adorjan, M. and Yau, H. L. (2015). "Resinicization and Digital Citizenship in Hong Kong: Youth, Au, K. L. (2017). *Twenty Shades of Freedom: Media Censorship Routines in Hong Kong*. Hong Kong: The Chinese University Press. [in Chinese]

Benecki, P. (2017). "Digging Deep." *The Maritime Executive*, September/October 2017, www.maritime-executive.com/magazine/digging-deep.

Bourdieu, P. (1991). *Language and Symbolic Power*. Cambridge, MA: Harvard University Press.

Bourdieu, P. and Wacquant, L. J. D. (1992). *An Invitation to Reflexive Sociology*. Chicago, IL: University of Chicago Press.

Bowe, A. (2018). *China's Overseas United Front Work: Background and Implications for the United States*. Washington, DC: US–China Economic and Security Review Commission.

Byler, D. (2021). *In the Camps: China's High Tech Penal Colony*. New York: Columbia Global Report.

Calabrese, J. (2013). "China and the Arab Awakening: The Cost of Doing Business." *China Report* 49, 1: 5–23.

Callahan, W. (2015). "Identity and Security in China: The Negative Soft Power of the China Dream." *Politics* 35, 3–4: 216–229.

Carroll, J. M. (2021). *The Hong Kong–China Nexus: A Brief History*. Cambridge: Cambridge University Press.

Chan, C. (2020). "Hong Kong Bankers Are Losing their Jobs to China Rivals." *Bloomberg News*, October 12, www.bloomberg.com/news/articles/2020-10-11/hong-kong-bankers-are-losing-their-jobs-to-mainland-china-rivals.

Chen, F. (2017). "Li Ruigang: China's Rupert Murdoch Comes to Hong Kong." *Hong Kong Economic Journal*, May 27, www.ejinsight.com/eji/article/id/1572404/20170526-li-ruigang-china-s-rupert-murdoch-comes-to-hong-kong.

Chen, K. (2020). "Sovereign Debt in the Making: Financial Entanglements and Labor Politics along the *Belt and Road* in Laos." *Economic Geography* 96, 4: 295–314.

Chen, K. (2022). "Harden the Hardline, Soften the Softline: Unravelling China's Qiaoling (侨领)-centred Diaspora Governance in Laos." *The China Quarterly* no. 250, June, 397–416.

Chen, T. C. (2010). "China's Reaction to the Color Revolutions." *Asian Perspective* 34, 2: 5–51.

Chen, Y. C. and Szeto, M. (2015). "The Forgotten Road of Progressive Localism: New Preservation Movement in Hong Kong." *Inter-Asia Cultural Studies* 16, 3: 436–453.

Cheng, E. W. (2020). "United Front Work and Mechanisms of Countermobilization in Hong Kong." *The China Journal* 83: 1–33.

Cheng, E. W. and Yuen, S., eds. (2018). *An Epoch of Social Movement: Trajectory of Contentious Politics in Hong Kong.* Hong Kong: Chinese University Press.

Cheng, Y. S. J. (2005). *The July 1 Protest Rally: Interpreting a Historic Event.* Hong Kong: City University of Hong Kong Press.

Cheung, S. K. (2014). "Reunification through Water and Food: The Other Battle for Lives and Bodies in China's Hong Kong Policy." *China Quarterly* 220: 1012–1032.

China.org. (2015). www.china.org.cn/english/china_key_words/2015-09/07/content_36528050.htm

Chui, S. and Hung, H. F. (1999). "State Building and Rural Stability," in T. W. Ngo (ed.), *Hong Kong's History: State and Society under Colonial Rule.* London, Routledge, 74–100.

Chui, S. and Liu, T. L. (2009). *Hong Kong: Becoming a Chinese Global City.* London: Routledge.

Corkin, L. (2013). *Uncovering African Agency: Angola's Management of China's Credit Lines.* London: Routledge.

De Kloet, J. (2018). "Umbrellas and Revolutions: The Aesthetics of the Hong Kong Protests," in E. Peeren et al. (eds.), *Global Cultures of Contestation.* London: Palgrave, 151–170.

Della Porta, D. (2012). "Eventful Protest, Global Conflicts: Social Mechanisms in the Reproduction of Protest," in J. Goodwin and J. Jasper (eds.), *Contention in Context: Political Opportunities and the Emergence of Protest.* Stanford, CA: Stanford University Press, 256–276.

Diamond, L. and Schell, O., eds. (2019) *China's Influence & American Interests: Promoting Constructive Vigilance.* Stanford, CA: Hoover Institution Press.

Dreher, A., A. Fuchs, R. Hodler, B. C. Parks, P. A. Raschky, and M. J. Tierney. (2019). "African Leaders and the Geography of China's Foreign Assistance." *Journal of Development Economics* 140: 44–71.

Fong, B. C. H. (2014). "The Partnership between the Chinese Government and Hong Kong's Capitalist Class." *China Quarterly* 217: 195–220.

Fong, B. C. H. (2017). "One Country, Two Nationalisms: Center-Periphery Relations between Mainland China and Hong Kong, 1997–2016." *Modern China* 43, 5: 523–556.

Fordahl, C. (2018). "Sovereignty and Martyrdom: A Sociological Sketch." *Journal of Historical Sociology* 31, 3: 297–313.

Goldstein, M. C. (1997). *The Snow Lion and the Dragon: China, Tibet, and the Dalai Lama*. Berkeley: University of California Press.

Goodstadt, L. F. (2009). *Uneasy Partners: The Conflict between Public Interest and Private Profit in Hong Kong*. Hong Kong: Hong Kong University Press.

Goodstadt, L. F. (2018). *A City Mismanaged: Hong Kong's Struggle for Survival*. Hong Kong: Hong Kong University Press.

Greitens, S. C. (2019). "Domestic Security in China under Xi Jinping." *China Leadership Monitor*, Spring, No. 59.

Greitens, S. C. (2021). "How Does China Think about National Security?" in A. J. Rudolph and M. Szonyi (eds.), *The China Questions II: Critical Insights into the US–China Relationship*. Cambridge, MA: Harvard University Press.

Greitens, S. C., Lee, M. and Yazici, E. (2020). "Counterterrorism and Preventive Repression and China's Changing Strategy in Xinjiang." *International Security* 44, 3: 9–47.

Gutiérrez, R. A. (2004). "Internal Colonialism: An American Theory of Race." *Du Bois Review* 1, 2: 281–295.

Hamilton, C. (2018). *Silent Invasion: China's Influence in Australia*. South Yarra: Hardie Grant Books.

Hamilton, E. P. (2021). *Made in Hong Kong: Transpacific Networks and a New History of Globalization*. New York: Columbia University Press.

Hamilton, G. G. (1999). *Cosmopolitan Capitalists: Hong Kong and the Chinese Diaspora at the End of the Twentieth Century*. Seattle: University of Washington Press.

He, B. (2019). "The Domestic Politics of the Belt and Road Initiative and its Implications." *Journal of Contemporary China* 28, 116: 180–195.

Hechter, M. (1975). *Internal Colonialism: The Celtic Fringe in British National Development, 1536–1966*. Berkeley: University of California Press.

Hirschman, A. O. (1945). *National Power and the Structure of Foreign Trade*. Berkeley: University of California Press.

Ho, J. (2004). "Lobbying under Way to Secure WTO Talks." *South China Morning Post*, February 28.

Ho, O. (2019). "Protest Art, Hong Kong Style: A Photo Essay," in C. K. Lee and M. Sing (eds.), *Take Back Our Future: An Eventful Sociology of the Hong Kong Umbrella Movement*. Ithaca, NY: Cornell University Press.

Hubbert, J. (2019). *China in the World: An Anthropology of Confucius Institutes, Soft Power, and Globalization*. Honolulu: University of Hawai'i Press.

Hui, P. K. (1999). "Comprador Politics and Middleman Capitalism," in T. W. Ngo (ed.), *Hong Kong's History: State and Society under Colonial Rule*. New York: Routledge, 30–45.

Hui, P. K., and Lau, K. C. (2015). "'Living in Truth' vs Realpolitik: Limitations and Potentials of the Umbrella Movement." *Inter-Asia Cultural Studies* 16, 3: 348–366.

Hung, H. F. (2008). "Rise of China and the Global Overaccumulation Crisis." *Review of International Political Economy* 15, 2: 149–179.

Hung, H. F. (2018). "China's State Capitalism and Its Discontents in Hong Kong." Paper presented at the Association for Asian Studies Annual Meeting, Washington D.C., March 22–25.

Hung, H. F. (2020). "The Periphery in the Making of Globalization: The China Lobby and the Reversal of Clinton's China Trade Policy, 1993–1994. *Review of International Political Economy*, published online. https://doi.org/10.1080/09692290.2020.1749105.

Jardine, B., Khashimov, S., Lemon, E., and Kyzy, A. U. (2020). *Mapping Patterns of Dissent in Eurasia*. The Oxus Society for Central Asia Affairs. https://oxussociety.org/wp-content/uploads/2020/10/2020-09-28-mapping-patterns-of-dissent-in-eurasia.pdf.

Jones, L. and Zeng, J. (2019). "Understanding China's 'Belt and Road Initiative': Beyond 'Grand Strategy' to a State Transformation Analysis." *Third World Quarterly* 40, 8: 1415–1439.

Kelly, D. (2017). "The 'China Solution': Beijing Responds to Trump." www.lowyinstitute.org/the-interpreter/china-solution-beijing-responds-trump.

Kwong, B. K. K. (2009). *Patron-Client Politics and Elections in Hong Kong*. London: Routledge.

Kwong, Y. H. (2016). "The Growth of 'Localism' in Hong Kong: A New Path for the Democracy Movement?" *China Perspectives* 3: 63–68.

Kygne, J. (2017). "Inside China's Secret 'Magic Weapon' for Worldwide Influence." *Financial Times*, October 25. www.ft.com/content/fb2b3934-b004-11e7-beba-5521c713abf4.

Lam, W.-M. (2004). *Understanding the Political Culture of Hong Kong*. Armonk: M.E. Sharpe.

Lam, W. W.-L. (1998). "The Chinese Government's Post-1997 Strategies," in Ian Scott (ed.), *Institutional Change and the Political Transition in Hong Kong*. London: Macmillan, 183–209.

Lam, Y. C. (2015). Choi Yuen Village Land Resumption and Anti-Express Rail Link Movement in Hong Kong: A Study of New Social Movements. M.Phil Thesis, Hong Kong University of Science and Technology.

Lau, S. K. (1982). *Society and Politics in Hong Kong*. Hong Kong: Chinese University of Hong Kong Press.

Lau, T. C. S., Tse, T. K. C., and Leung, Y. W. (2016). "Dynamics of Chinese Nationalistic Education in Hong Kong from 1945 to 2012." *Oxford Review of Education* 42, 6;, 677–691.

Law, W. S. (2017). "Decolonization Deferred," in W. M. Lam and L. Cooper (eds.), *Citizenship, Identity and Social Movements in the New Hong Kong: Localism after the Umbrella Movement*. London Routledge.

Lee, C. K. 2017. *The Specter of Global China: Politics, Labor and Foreign Investment in Africa*. Chicago: University of Chicago Press.

Lee, C. K. and Zhang, Y. H. (2013). "The Power of Instability: Unraveling the Microfoundations of Bargained Authoritarianism in China." *American Journal of Sociology* 118, 6: 1475–1508.

Lee, E. W. Y. (2020). "United Front, Clientelism, and Indirect Rule: Theorizing the Role of the 'Liaison Office' in Hong Kong." *Journal of Contemporary China* 29, 763–775.

Lee, F. L. F. (2018). "Changing Political Economy of the Hong Kong Media." *China Perspectives* 3: 9–18.

Lee, F. L. F. (2020). "Solidarity in the Anti-Extradition Bill Movement." *Critical Asian Studies* 52, 1: 18–32.

Lee, F. L. F. and Chan, J. M. (2008). "Making Sense of Participation: The Political Culture of Pro-democracy Demonstrators in Hong Kong." *China Quarterly* 193, 84–101.

Lee, F. L. F., and Chan, J. M. (2011). *Media, Social Mobilisation and Mass Protests in Post-Colonial Hong Kong: The Power of a Critical Event*. London: Routledge.

Lee, F. L. F and Chan, J. M. (2018). *Media and Protest Logics in the Digital Era: The Umbrella Movement in Hong Kong*. New York: Oxford University Press.

Lim, T. W. (2015). "The Aesthetics of Hong Kong's 'Umbrella Revolution' in the First Ten Days." *East Asia* 32: 83–98.

Lui, T.-L. (2007). *Four Generations of Hong Kong People*. Hong Kong: Stepforward. [in Chinese]

Lui, T.-L. and Chiu, S. W. K. (2007). "Governance Crisis in Post-1997 Hong Kong: A Political Economy Perspective." *China Review* 7, 2: 1–34.

Lui, T.-L. and Chiu, S. W. K. (2014). 胸懷祖國：香港「愛國左派」運動. Hong Kong: Oxford University Press.

Lumumba-Kasongo, T. (2011). "China-Africa Relations: A Neo-Imperialism or a Neo-Colonialism? A Reflection." *African and Asian Studies* 10: 234–266.

Lu, J. (2022). "For Profit or Patriotism? The limitations and benefits of state support for a Chinese state-owned rubber firm in Laos," *The China Quarterly* no. 250, June, 332–355.

Ma, N. (2007). *Political Development in Hong Kong: State, Political Society and Civil Society in Hong Kong*. Hong Kong: Hong Kong University Press.

Ma, N. (2015). "The Rise of "Anti-China" Sentiments in Hong Kong and the 2012 Legislative Council Elections." *China Review* 15, 1: 39–66.

Ma, N. (2016). "The Making of a Corporatist State in Hong Kong: The Road to Sectoral Intervention." *Journal of Contemporary Asia* 46, 2: 247–266.

Ma, N. and Cheng, E. W. eds. (2019). *The Umbrella Movement: Civil Resistance and Contentious Space in Hong Kong*. Amsterdam: Amsterdam University Press.

Mahoney, J. (2012). *Colonialism and Postcolonial Development*. Cambridge: Cambridge University Press.

Man, L. K. W. (2017). "Artistic Activism," in J. Luger and J. Ren (eds.), *Art and the City: Worlding the Discussion through a Critical Artscape*. London: Taylor & Francis 115–127.

Mannheim, K. (1952). "The Problem of Generations," in *Essays on the Sociology of Knowledge*. London: Routledge and Kegan Paul, 276–320 [first published 1923].

Marx, K. 1992 [1867] Capital: A Critique of Political Economy. Volume 1. London: Penguin Books.

McAdam, D. and Sewell, W. H., Jr. (2001). "It's About Time: Temporality in the Study of Social Movements and Revolutions," in R. Aminzade et al. (eds.), *Silence and Voice in the Study of Contentious Politics*. Cambridge: Cambridge University Press, 89–125.

Morris, P. and Vickers, E. (2015). "Schooling, Politics and the Construction of Identity in Hong Kong: The 2012 'Moral and National Education' Crisis in Historical Context." *Comparative Education* 51, 3: 305–326.

Naughton, B. (1999). "Between China and the World: Hong Kong's Economy before and after 1997," in G. Hamilton (ed.), *Cosmopolitan Capitalists: Hong Kong and the Chinese Diaspora*. Seattle: University of Washington Press 80–99.

Ng, V. and Chan, K. M. (2017). "Emotion Politics: Joyous Resistance in Hong Kong." *China Review* 17, 1: 83–115.

Ngo, T. W. (2019). "A Genealogy of Business and Politics in Hong Kong," in T.-l. Lui, S. W. K. Chiu, and R. Yep (eds.), *Routledge Handbook of Contemporary Hong Kong*. London: Routledge, 324–341.

Norris, W. J. (2016). *Chinese Economic Statecraft: Commercial Actors, Grand Strategy, and State Control*. Ithaca, NY: Cornell University Press.

Patey, L. (2014). *The New Kings of Crude: China, India, and the Global Struggle for Oil in Sudan and South Sudan*. London: Hurst.

Petersen, C. J. (2005). "Hong Kong's Spring of Discontent: The Rise and Fall of the National Security Bill in 2003," in F. Hualing, C. J. Petersen and S. N. M. Young (eds.), *National Security and Fundamental Freedom*. Hong Kong: Hong Kong University Press.

Pilcher, J. (1994). "Mannheim's Sociology of Generations: An Undervalued Legacy." *British Journal of Sociology* 45, 3: 481–495.

Polanyi, K. ([1944] 2001). *The Great Transformation: The Political and Economic Origins of Our Time*. 2nd ed. Boston: Beacon Press.

Public Opinion Program. (2019). "HKU POP Final Farewell: Rift Widens between Chinese and Hongkong Identities, National Chief Plunges to One in Four," June 27, www.hkupop.hku.hk/english/release/release1594.html.

Quiliconi, C. and Vasco, P. R. (2021). *Chinese Mining and Indigenous Resistance in Ecuador*. Washington, DC: Carnegie Endowment for International Peace.

Reguly, E. (2019). "China's Piraeus Power Play." *The Globe and Mail*, July 7, www.theglobeandmail.com/world/article-chinas-piraeus-power-play-in-greece-a-port-project-offers-beijing/.

Repnikova, M. "Rethinking China's Soft Power: 'Pragmatic Enticement' of Confucius Institutes in Ethiopia." The China Quarterly no. 250, June, 440–463.

Roberts, P. (2016). "Cold War Hong Kong: Juggling Opposing Forces and identities," in P. Roberts and J. M. Carroll (eds.), *Hong Kong in the Cold War*. Hong Kong: Hong Kong University Press, 26–59.

Sassen, S. (2001). *The Global City: New York, London, Tokyo*, revised ed. Princeton, NJ: Princeton University Press.

Schiffer, J. R. (1991). "State Policy and Economic Growth: A Note on the Hong Kong Model." *International Journal of Urban and Regional Research* 15, 2: 180–196.

Schmidt, B. (2020). "The Publishing Empire Helping China Silence Dissent in Hong Kong." *Japan Times*, August 18, www.japantimes.co.jp/news/2020/08/18/asia-pacific/politics-diplomacy-asia-pacific/publishing-china-hong-kong-media/.

Scott, I. (1989). *Political Change and the Crisis of Legitimacy in Hong Kong*. Hong Kong: Oxford University Press.

Sewell, W., Jr. (1996). "Historical Events as Transformation of Structure." *Theory and Society* 25, 6: 841–881.

Sewell, W., Jr. (2005). "Three Temporalities: Toward an Eventful Sociology," in *Logics of History: Social Theory and Social Transformation*. Chicago: University of Chicago Press, 81–123.

South China Morning Post, (2000) Editorial. October 26.

Stott, C., Ho, L., Radburn, M., Chan, Y. T., Kyprianides, A., and Morales, P. S. (2020). "Patterns of 'Disorder' during the 2019 Protests in Hong Kong: Policing, Social Identity, Intergroup Dynamics, and Radicalization." *Policing* 14, 4: 814–835.

To, J. J. H. (2014). *Qiaowu: Extra-territorial Policies for the Overseas Chinese.* Leiden, Netherlands: Brill.

The Guardian, July 24, 2020. www.theguardian.com/world/2020/jul/24/mike-pompeo-says-free-world-must-change-china-or-china-will-change-us (accessed August 15, 2020).

Tse, T. K. C. (2007). "Remaking Chinese Identity: Hegemonic Struggles over National Education in Post-Colonial Hong Kong." *International Studies in Sociology of Education* 17, 3: 231–248.

Tsui, E. S. Y. (2017). 思索家邦：中國殖民主義狂潮下的香港. Taipei: Avanguard Press. [in Chinese]

Veg, S. (2017). "The Rise of 'Localism' and Civic Identity in Post-Handover Hong Kong: Questioning the Chinese Nation-State." *The China Quarterly* 230: 323–347.

Veg, S. (2019). "The Rise of China's Statist Intellectuals: Law, Sovereignty, and 'Repolicitization.'" *The China Journal* 82: 23–45.

Walder, A. (2009). "Political Sociology and Social Movements." *Annual Review of Sociology* 35: 393–412.

Washington Post. (2000). "Discontent Afflicts Hong Kong: Protest Epidemic Reflects Rising Anxiety of Middle Class," June 28, A21.

Watkins, D. (2015). "What China Has Been Building in the South China Sea." *New York Times*, October 27.

Wong, J. (2015). "Scholarism on the March." *New Left Review* March-April, 43–52.

Wong, S. H. W, Ma, N., and Lam, W.M. (2016). "Migrants and Democratization: The Political Economy of Chinese Immigrants in Hong Kong." *Contemporary Chinese Political Economy and Strategic Relations: An International Journal* 2, 2: 909–940.

Wong, S. H. W, Ma, N., and Lam, W. M. (2018). "Immigrants as Voters in Electoral Autocracies: The Case of Mainland Chinese Immigrants in Hong Kong." *Journal of East Asian Studies* 18, 1 67–95.

Wong, Y. C. (2006)."'Super Paradox' or 'Leninist Integration': Tthe Politics of Legislating Article 23 of Hong Kong's Basic Law." *Asian Perspective* 30, 2: 65–95.

Wu, J. M. (2015). "The Path to the Sunflower Movement: How the Taiwanese Civil Society Has Resisted the China Factor." *Nihon Taiwan Gakkaihou* No. 17. [in Chinese]

Wu, J. M. (2019). "Taiwan's Sunflower Occupy Movement as a Transformative Resistance to the 'China Factor,'" in C. K. Lee, and M. Sing (eds)., *Take Back Our Future: An Eventful Sociology of the Hong Kong Umbrella Movement*. Ithaca, NY: Cornell University Press, 215–240.

Yang, C. (2006). "The Geopolitics of Cross-Boundary Governance in the Great Pearl River Delta, China: A Case Study of the Proposed Hong Kong-Zhuhai-Macao Bridge." *Political Geography* 25: 817–835.

Yang, X. (2019). "Hong Kong-Zhuhai-Macao Bridge Introduces Chinese Standards to the World." *People's Daily*, March 15, http://en.people.cn/n3/ 2019/0315/c90000-9556631.html.

Yang, Y. E. and Liang, W. (2019). "Introduction to China's Economic Statecraft: Rising Influences, Mixed Results." *Journal of Chinese Political Science* 24: 381–385.

Yeh, E. and Wharton, E. (2016). "Going West and Going Out: Discourses, Migrants, and Models in Chinese Development." *Eurasian Geography and Economics* 57:3, 286–315.

Yuen, S. (2021). "The Institutional Foundation of Countermobilization: Elites and Pro-Regime Grassroots Organizations in Post-Handover Hong Kong." *Government and Opposition* 1–22.

Yuen, S and Chung, S. (2018). "Explaining Localism in Post-handover Hong Kong." *China Perspectives* 3: 19–29.

Zhang, H. (2020). "The Aid-Contracting Nexus: The Role of the International Contracting Industry in China's Overseas Development Engagements." *China Perspectives* 4: 17–27.

Cambridge Elements ᵿ

Global China

Ching Kwan Lee

University of California–Los Angeles

Ching Kwan Lee is Professor of Sociology at the University of California–Los Angeles. Her scholarly interests include political sociology, popular protests, labor, development, political economy, comparative ethnography, China, Hong Kong, East Asia, and the Global South. She is the author of three multiple award-winning monographs on contemporary China: *Gender and the South China Miracle: Two Worlds of Factory Women* (1998), *Against the Law: Labor Protests in China's Rustbelt and Sunbelt* (2007), and *The Specter of Global China: Politics, Labor and Foreign Investment in Africa* (2017). Her coedited volumes include *Take Back Our Future: an Eventful Sociology of Hong Kong's Umbrella Movement* (2019) and *The Social Question in the 21st Century: A Global View* (2019).

About the series

The Cambridge Elements series Global China showcases thematic, region- or country-specific studies on China's multifaceted global engagements and impacts. Each title, written by a leading scholar of the subject matter at hand, combines a succinct, comprehensive and up-to-date overview of the debates in the scholarly literature with original analysis and a clear argument. Featuring cutting edge scholarship on arguably one of the most important and controversial developments in the 21st century, the Global China Elements series will advance a new direction of China scholarship that expands China Studies beyond China's territorial boundaries.

Cambridge Elements ≡

Global China

Elements in the series

Printed in the United States
by Baker & Taylor Publisher Services